The Story of My Life

AF819382

The Story of My Life

Helen Keller

PRABHAT
PAPERBACKS

No part of this publication can be reproduced, stored in a retrieval system or transmitted in any form or by any means, electronic, mechanical, photocopying, recording or otherwise, without the prior permission of the author and the publisher.

Published by
PRABHAT PAPERBACKS
An imprint of Prabhat Prakashan Pvt. Ltd.
4/19 Asaf Ali Road,
New Delhi-110002 (INDIA)
e-mail: prabhatbooks@gmail.com

ISBN 978-93-5186-414-1
The Story of My Life
by Helen Keller

© Reserved

Edition
2021

Price
₹ 250.00 (Rupees Two Hundred Fifty only)

Printed at
R-Tech Offset Printers, Delhi

To ALEXANDER GRAHAM BELL

Who has taught the deaf to speak
and enabled the listening ear to hear speech
from the Atlantic to the Rockies,
I dedicate
this Story of My Life.

1

It is with a kind of fear that I begin to write the history of my life. I have, as it were, a superstitious hesitation in lifting the veil that clings about my childhood like a golden mist. The task of writing an autobiography is a difficult one. When I try to classify my earliest impressions, I find that fact and fancy look alike across the years that link the past with the present. The woman paints the child's experiences in her own fantasy. A few impressions stand out vividly from the first years of my life; but "the shadows of the prison-house are on the rest." Besides, many of the joys and sorrows of childhood have lost their poignancy; and many incidents of vital importance in my early education have been forgotten in the excitement of great discoveries. In order, therefore, not to be tedious I shall try to present in a series of sketches only the episodes that seem to me to be the most interesting and important.

I was born on June 27, 1880, in Tuscumbia, a little town of northern Alabama.

The family on my father's side is descendent of Caspar Keller, a native of Switzerland, who settled in Maryland. One of my Swiss ancestors was the first teacher of the deaf in Zurich and wrote a book on the subject of their education—rather a singular coincidence; though it is true that there is no king who has not had a slave among his ancestors, and no slave who has not had a king among his.

My grandfather, Caspar Keller's son, "entered" large tracts of land in Alabama and finally settled there. I have been told that once a year he went from Tuscumbia to Philadelphia on horseback to purchase supplies for the plantation, and my aunt has in her possession many of the letters to his family, which give charming and vivid accounts of these trips.

My Grandmother Keller was a daughter of one of Lafayette's aides, Alexander Moore, and granddaughter of Alexander Spotswood, an early Colonial Governor of Virginia. She was also second cousin to Robert E. Lee.

My father, Arthur H. Keller, was a captain in the Confederate Army, and my mother, Kate Adams, was his second wife and many years younger. Her grandfather, Benjamin Adams, married Susanna E. Goodhue, and lived in Newbury, Massachusetts, for many years. Their son, Charles Adams, was born in Newburyport, Massachusetts, and moved to Helena, Arkansas. When the Civil War broke out, he fought on the side of the South and became a brigadier-general. He married Lucy Helen Everett, who belonged to the same family of Everetts as Edward Everett and Dr. Edward Everett Hale. After the war was over, the family moved to Memphis, Tennessee.

My father, Arthur H. Keller, was a captain in the Confederate Army, and my mother, Kate Adams, was his second wife and many years younger. Her grandfather, Benjamin Adams, married Susanna E. Goodhue, and lived in Newbury, Massachusetts, for many years.

I lived, up to the time of the illness that deprived me of my sight and hearing, in a tiny house consisting of a large square room and a small one, in which the servant slept. It is a custom in the South to build a small house near the homestead as an annexe to be used on special occasions. My father built such a house after the Civil War, and when he married my mother they went to live in it. It was completely covered with vines, climbing roses and honeysuckles. From the garden it looked like an arbour. The little porch was hidden from view by a screen of yellow roses and Southern smilax. It was the favourite haunt of humming-birds and bees.

The Keller homestead, where the family lived, was a few steps from our little rose-bower. It was called "Ivy Green" because the house and the surrounding trees and fences were covered with beautiful English ivy. Its old-fashioned garden was the paradise of my childhood.

Even in the days before my teacher came, I used to feel along the square stiff boxwood hedges, and, guided by the sense of smell would find the first violets and lilies. It was there that I went to find comfort and to hide my hot face in the cool leaves and grass after a fit of temper.

Even in the days before my teacher came, I used to feel along the square stiff boxwood hedges, and, guided by the sense of smell would find the first violets and lilies. It was there that I went to find comfort and to hide my hot face in the cool leaves and grass after a fit of temper. What joy it was to lose myself in that garden of flowers, to wander happily from spot to spot, until, coming suddenly upon a beautiful vine, I recognised it by its leaves and blossoms, and knew it was the vine which covered the tumble-down summer-house at the farther end of the garden! There were trailing clematis, drooping jessamine also and some rare sweet flowers called butterfly lilies, named so because their fragile petals that resembled butterflies' wings. But the roses—they were loveliest of all. Never have I found in the greenhouses of the North such heart-satisfying roses as the climbing roses of my Southern home. They used to hang in long festoons from our porch, filling the whole air with their fragrance, untainted by any earthy smell; and in the early morning, washed in the dew, they felt so soft, so pure, I could not help wondering if they did not resemble the asphodels of God's garden.

The beginning of my life was simple and much like every other little life. I came, I saw, I conquered, as the first baby in the family always does. There was the usual amount of discussion as to a name for me. The first baby in the family was not to be lightly named; everyone was emphatic about that.

The beginning of my life was simple and much like every other little life. I came, I saw, I conquered, as the first baby in the family always does. There was the usual amount of discussion as to a name for me. The first baby in the family was not to be lightly named; everyone was emphatic about that. My father suggested the name of Mildred Campbell, an ancestor whom he highly esteemed, and he declined to take any further part in the discussion. My mother solved the problem by giving it as her wish that I should be called after her mother, whose maiden name was Helen Everett. But in the excitement of carrying me to church my father lost the name on the way, very naturally, since it was one in which he had declined to have a part. When the minister asked him for it, he just remembered that it had been decided that I was to be named after my grandmother, and so he gave her name as Helen Adams.

I am told that while I was still in long dresses I showed many signs of an eager, self-asserting disposition. I insisted upon imitating everything that I saw other people do. At six months I could pipe out "How d'ye," and one day I attracted everyone's attention by saying "Tea, tea, tea" quite plainly. Even after my illness I remembered one of the words I had learnt in these early months. It was the word "water," and I continued to make some sound for that word after all other speech was lost. I ceased making the sound "wah-wah" only when I learnt to spell the word.

They tell me I walked the day I was a year old. My mother had just taken me out of the bath-tub and was holding me in her lap, when I was suddenly attracted by the flickering shadows of leaves that danced in the sunlight on the smooth floor. I slipped from my mother's lap and almost ran towards them. Once the impulse was gone, I fell down and cried for her to take me up in her arms.

My mother had just taken me out of the bath-tub and was holding me in her lap, when I was suddenly attracted by the flickering shadows of leaves that danced in the sunlight on the smooth floor. I slipped from my mother's lap and almost ran towards them. Once the impulse was gone, I fell down and cried for her to take me up in her arms.

These happy days did not last long. One brief spring, musical with the song of robin and mocking-bird, one summer rich in fruit and roses, one autumn of gold and crimson sped by and left their gifts at the feet of an eager, delighted child. Then, in the dreary month of February, came the illness which closed my eyes and ears and plunged me into the unconsciousness of a new-born baby. They called it acute congestion of the stomach and brain. The doctor thought that I would not live. Early one morning, however, the fever left me as suddenly and mysteriously as it had come. There was great rejoicing in the family that morning, but no one, not even the doctor, knew that I would never see or hear again.

I fancy I still have confused recollections of that illness. I especially remember the tenderness with which my mother tried to soothe me in my waking hours of fret and pain, and the agony and bewilderment with which I awoke after a disturbed half sleep, and turned my eyes, so dry and hot, to the wall away from the once-loved light, which came to me dim and yet dimmer each day. But, except for these fleeting memories, if, indeed, they be memories, it all seems very unreal, like a nightmare. Gradually I got used to the silence and darkness that surrounded me and forgot that it had ever been different, until she came—my teacher—who was to set

I fancy I still have confused recollections of that illness. I especially remember the tenderness with which my mother tried to soothe me in my waking hours of fret and pain, and the agony and bewilderment with which I awoke after a disturbed half sleep, and turned my eyes, so dry and hot, to the wall away from the once-loved light, which came to me dim and yet dimmer each day.

my spirit free. However, during the first nineteen months of my life I had caught glimpses of broad, green fields, a luminous sky, trees and flowers which the darkness that followed could not wholly blot out. If we have once seen, "the day is ours, and also what the day has shown."

□

2

I cannot recall what happened during the first months after my illness. I only know that I sat in my mother's lap or clung to her dress as she went about her household duties. My hands felt every object and observed every motion, and in this way I learnt to know many things. Soon I felt the need of some communication with others and began to make crude signs. A shake of the head meant "No" and a nod, "Yes," a pull meant "Come" and a push, "Go." If it was bread that I wanted, then I would imitate the acts of cutting the slices and buttering them. If I wanted my mother to make ice-cream for dinner I made the sign for working the freezer and shivered, indicating cold. My mother, moreover, succeeded in making me understand a good deal. I always knew when she wished me to bring her something, and I would run upstairs or anywhere else she indicated. Indeed, I owe to her loving wisdom all that was bright and good in my long night.

I understood a good deal of what was going on about me. At five I had learnt to fold and put away the clean clothes when they were brought in from the laundry, and I could distinguish my own from the rest. I knew by the way my mother and aunt dressed when they were going out, and I invariably begged to go with them. I was always sent for when there was company, and when the guests took their leave, I waved my hand at them, I think with a vague remembrance of the meaning of the gesture. One day some gentlemen called on my mother, and I felt the shutting of the front door and other sounds that indicated their arrival. On a sudden thought I ran upstairs before anyone could stop me, to put on my idea of a company dress. Standing before the mirror, as I had seen others do, I anointed my head with oil and covered my face thickly with powder. Then I pinned a veil over my head so that it covered my face and fell in folds down to my shoulders, and tied an enormous bustle round my small waist, so that it dangled behind, almost meeting the hem of my skirt. Thus attired I went down to help entertain the company.

I do not remember when I first realised that I was different from other people; but I knew it before my teacher came to me. I had noticed that my mother and my friends did not use signs as I did when they wanted anything done, but talked with their mouths.

I do not remember when I first realised that I was different from other people; but I knew it before my teacher came to me. I had noticed that my mother and my friends did not use signs as I did when they wanted anything done, but talked with their mouths. Sometimes I stood between two persons who were conversing and touched their lips. I could not understand, and was vexed. I moved my lips and gesticulated frantically without result. This made me so angry at times that I kicked and screamed until I was exhausted.

I think I knew when I was naughty, for I knew that it hurt Ella, my nurse, if I kicked her, and when my fit of temper was over I had a feeling akin to regret. But I cannot remember any instance in which this feeling prevented me from repeating the naughtiness when I failed to get what I wanted.

In those days a little coloured girl, Martha Washington, the child of our cook, and Belle, an old setter, and a great hunter in her day, were my constant companions. Martha Washington understood my signs, and I seldom had any difficulty in making her do just as I wished. It pleased me to domineer over her, and she generally submitted to my tyranny rather than risk a hand-to-hand encounter. I was strong, active and indifferent to consequences. I knew my own mind well enough and always had my own way, even if I had to fight tooth and nail for it. We spent a great deal of time in the kitchen, kneading dough balls, helping make ice-cream, grinding coffee, quarrelling over the cake-bowl, and feeding the hens and turkeys that swarmed about on the kitchen steps. Many of them were so tame that they would eat from my hand and let me feel them. One big gobbler snatched a tomato from me one day and ran away with it. Inspired, perhaps, by Master Gobbler's success, we carried off to the woodpile a cake which the cook had just frosted, and ate every bit of it. I was quite ill afterwards, and I wonder if retribution also overtook the turkey.

In those days a little coloured girl, Martha Washington, the child of our cook, and Belle, an old setter, and a great hunter in her day, were my constant companions. Martha Washington understood my signs, and I seldom had any difficulty in making her do just as I wished.

The guinea-fowl likes to hide her nest in out-of-the-way places, and it was one of my greatest delights to hunt for the eggs in the long grass. I could not tell Martha Washington when I wanted to go egg-hunting, but I would cup my hands and put them on the ground, which meant something round in the grass, and Martha always understood. When we were fortunate enough to find a nest I never allowed her to carry the eggs home, making her understand by emphatic signs that she might drop and break them.

The sheds where the corn was stored, the stable where the horses were kept, and the yard where the cows were milked morning and evening, were unfailing sources of interest to Martha and me. The milk men would let me keep my hands on the cows while they milked, and I often got well switched by the cows for my curiosity.

The sheds where the corn was stored, the stable where the horses were kept, and the yard where the cows were milked morning and evening, were unfailing sources of interest to Martha and me. The milk men would let me keep my hands on the cows while they milked, and I often got well switched by the cows for my curiosity.

The preparations for Christmas were always a delight to me. Of course I did not know what it was all about, but I enjoyed the pleasant odours that filled the house and the titbits that were given to Martha Washington and me to keep us quiet. We were sadly in the way, but that did not interfere with our pleasure in the least. They allowed us to grind the spices, pick over the raisins and lick the stirring spoons. I hung my stocking because the others did; I cannot remember, however, that the ceremony interested me especially, nor did my curiosity cause me to wake before daylight to look for my gifts.

Martha Washington had as great a love of mischief as I. Two little children were seated on the veranda steps one hot

July afternoon. One was black as ebony, with little bunches of fuzzy hair tied with shoestrings sticking out all over her head like corkscrews. The other was white, with long golden curls. One child was six years old, the other two or three years older. The younger child was blind—that was I—and the other was Martha Washington. We were busy cutting out paper dolls; but we soon wearied of this amusement, and after cutting up our shoestrings and clipping all the leaves off the honeysuckle that were within reach, I turned my attention to Martha's corkscrews. She objected at first, but finally submitted. Thinking that turn and turn about is fair play, she seized the scissors and cut off one of my curls, and would have cut them all off but for my mother's timely interference.

Belle, our dog, my other companion, was old and lazy and liked to sleep by the open fire rather than to romp with me. I tried hard to teach her my sign language, but she was dull and inattentive. She sometimes started and quivered with excitement and then she became perfectly rigid, as dogs do when they concentrate on a bird.

Belle, our dog, my other companion, was old and lazy and liked to sleep by the open fire rather than to romp with me. I tried hard to teach her my sign language, but she was dull and inattentive. She sometimes started and quivered with excitement and then she became perfectly rigid, as dogs do when they concentrate on a bird. I did not then know why Belle acted in this way; but I knew she was not doing as I wished. This vexed me and the lesson always ended in a one-sided boxing match. Belle would get up, stretch herself lazily, give one or two contemptuous sniffs, go to the opposite side of the hearth and lie down again, and I, wearied and disappointed, would go off in search of Martha.

Many incidents of those early years are fixed in my memory, isolated, but clear and distinct, making the sense of that silent, aimless, day less life all the more intense.

One day I happened to spill water on my apron, and I spread it out to dry before the fire which was flickering on the sitting-room hearth. The apron did not dry quickly enough to suit me, so I drew nearer and threw it right over the hot ashes. The fire leaped into life; the flames encircled me so that in a moment my clothes were blazing. I made a terrified noise that brought Viny, my old nurse, to the rescue. Throwing a blanket over me, she almost suffocated me, but she put out the fire. Except for my hands and hair I was not badly burnt.

One day I happened to spill water on my apron, and I spread it out to dry before the fire which was flickering on the sitting-room hearth. The apron did not dry quickly enough to suit me, so I drew nearer and threw it right over the hot ashes.

About this time I found out the use of a key. One morning I locked my mother up in the pantry, where she was obliged to remain for three hours, as the servants were in a detached part of the house. She kept pounding on the door, while I sat outside on the porch steps and laughed with glee as I felt the jar of the pounding. This most naughty prank of mine convinced my parents that I must be taught as soon as possible. After my teacher, Miss Sullivan, came to me, I sought an early opportunity to lock her in her room. I went upstairs with something which my mother made me understand I was to give to Miss Sullivan; but no sooner had I given it to her than I slammed the door too, locked it, and hid the key under the wardrobe in the hall. I could not be induced to tell where the key was. My father was obliged to get a ladder and take Miss Sullivan out through the window—much to my delight. Months after I produced the key.

When I was about five years old, we moved from the little vine-covered house to a large new one. My family consisted of my father and mother, two older half-brothers, and, afterwards, a little sister, Mildred. My earliest distinct recollection of my father is of making my way through great drifts of newspapers to his side and finding him alone, holding a sheet of paper before his face. I was greatly puzzled to know what he was doing. I imitated this action, even wearing his spectacles, thinking they might help solve the mystery. But I did not find out the secret for several years. Then I learnt what those papers were, and that my father edited one of them.

My father was most loving and indulgent, devoted to his home and seldom left us, except in the hunting season. He was a great hunter, I have been told, and a celebrated shot. Next to his family he loved his dogs and gun. His hospitality was great, almost to a fault, and he seldom came home without bringing a guest.

My father was most loving and indulgent, devoted to his home and seldom left us, except in the hunting season. He was a great hunter, I have been told, and a celebrated shot. Next to his family he loved his dogs and gun. His hospitality was great, almost to a fault, and he seldom came home without bringing a guest. His special pride was the big garden where, it was said, he raised the finest watermelons and strawberries in the county; and to me he brought the first ripe grapes and the choicest berries. I remember his caressing touch as he led me from tree to tree, from vine to vine, and his eager delight in whatever pleased me.

He was a famous story-teller and after I had acquired language, he used to spell clumsily into my hand his cleverest anecdotes, and nothing pleased him more than to have me repeat them at an opportune moment.

I was in the North, enjoying the last beautiful days of the summer of 1896, when I heard the news of my father's death. He had a short illness, there had been a brief time of acute suffering and then all was over. This was my first great sorrow—my first personal experience with death.

I was in the North, enjoying the last beautiful days of the summer of 1896, when I heard the news of my father's death. He had a short illness, there had been a brief time of acute suffering and then all was over. This was my first great sorrow—my first personal experience with death.

How shall I write of my mother? She is so near to me that it almost seems indelicate to speak of her.

For a long time I regarded my little sister as an intruder. I knew that I had ceased to be my mother's only darling, and the thought filled me with jealousy. She sat in my mother's lap constantly, where I used to sit, and seemed to take up all her care and time. One day something happened which seemed to me to be adding insult to injury.

At that time I had a much-petted, much-abused doll, which I afterwards named Nancy. She was, alas, the helpless victim of my outbursts of temper and of affection, so that she became much the worse for wear. I had dolls which talked, and cried, and opened and shut their eyes; yet I never loved one of them as I loved poor Nancy. She had a cradle, and I often spent an hour or more rocking her. I guarded both doll and cradle with the most jealous care; but once I discovered my little sister sleeping peacefully in the cradle. At this presumption on the part of one to whom as yet no tie of love bound me I grew angry. I rushed upon the cradle and over-turned it, and the baby might have been killed had my mother not caught her as she fell. Thus it is that when we walk in the valley of twofold solitude we know little of the tender affections that grow out of endearing words and actions and companionship. But afterwards, when I was restored to my human heritage, Mildred and I grew into each other's hearts, so that we were content to go hand-in-hand wherever caprice led us, although she could not understand my finger language, nor I her childish prattle.

□

3

Meanwhile, the desire to express myself grew. The few signs I used became less and less adequate, and my failures to make myself understood were invariably followed by outbursts of passion. I felt as if invisible hands were holding me, and I made frantic efforts to free myself. I struggled—not that struggling helped matters, but the spirit of resistance was strong within me. I generally broke down in tears and physical exhaustion. If my mother happened to be near I crept into her arms, too miserable even to remember the cause of the tempest. After a while, the need of some means of communication became so urgent that these outbursts occurred daily, sometimes hourly.

My parents were deeply grieved and perplexed. We lived a long way from any school for the blind or the deaf, and it seemed unlikely that anyone would come to such an out-of-the-way place as Tuscumbia to teach a child who was both deaf and blind. Indeed, my friends and relatives sometimes doubted whether I could be taught. My mother's only ray of hope came from Dickens's "American Notes." She had read his account of Laura Bridgman, and remembered vaguely that she was deaf and blind and yet had been educated. But she also remembered with a hopeless pang that Dr. Howe, who had discovered the way to teach the deaf and blind, had been dead for many years. His methods had probably died with him; and if they had not, how was a little girl in a far-off town in Alabama to receive the benefit of them?

When I was about six years old, my father heard of an eminent oculist in Baltimore, who had been successful in many cases that had seemed hopeless. My parents at once determined to take me to Baltimore to see if anything could be done for my eyes.

The journey, which I remember well, was very pleasant. I made friends with many people on the train. One lady gave me a box of shells. My father made holes in them so that I could string them, and for a long time they kept me happy and contented. The conductor, too, was kind. Often when he went on his rounds, I clung to his coat tails while he collected and punched the tickets. His punch, with which he let me play, was a delightful toy. Curled up in a corner of the seat, I amused myself for hours making funny little holes in bits of cardboard.

When I was about six years old, my father heard of an eminent oculist in Baltimore, who had been successful in many cases that had seemed hopeless. My parents at once determined to take me to Baltimore to see if anything could be done for my eyes.

My aunt made me a big doll out of towels. It was the most comical shapeless thing, with no nose, mouth, ears or eyes—nothing that even the imagination of a child could convert into a face. Curiously enough, the absence of eyes struck me more than all the other defects put together. I pointed this out to everybody with provoking persistency, but no one seemed able to provide the doll with eyes. A bright idea, however, shot into my mind, and the problem was solved. I tumbled off the seat and searched under it until I found my aunt's cape, which was trimmed with large beads.

I pulled two beads off and indicated to her that I wanted her to sew them on my doll. She raised my hand to her eyes in a questioning way, and I nodded energetically. The beads were sewed in the right place and I could not contain myself for joy; but immediately I lost all interest in the doll. During the whole trip I did not have one fit of temper for there were so many things to keep my mind and fingers busy.

When we arrived in Baltimore, Dr. Chisholm received us kindly, but he could do nothing. He said, however, that I could be educated, and advised my father to consult Dr. Alexander Graham Bell of Washington, who would be able to give him information about schools and teachers of deaf or blind children. Acting on the doctor's advice, we went immediately to Washington to see Dr. Bell; my father with a sad heart and many misgivings, I wholly unconscious of his anguish, finding pleasure in the excitement of moving from place to place. Child as I was, I once felt the tenderness and sympathy which endeared Dr. Bell to so many hearts, as his wonderful achievements enlisted their admiration. He held me on his knee while I examined his watch, and he made it strike for me. He understood my signs, and I knew it and loved him at once. However, I did not have even the faintest idea that interview would be the door through which I would pass from darkness into light, from isolation to friendship,

When we arrived in Baltimore, Dr. Chisholm received us kindly, but he could do nothing. He said, however, that I could be educated, and advised my father to consult Dr. Alexander Graham Bell of Washington, who would be able to give him information about schools and teachers of deaf or blind children.

companionship, knowledge and love.

Dr. Bell advised my father to write to Mr. Anagnos, director of the Perkins Institution in Boston, the scene of Dr. Howe's great labour for the blind, and ask him if he had a teacher competent to begin my education. This my father did at once, and in a few weeks there came a kind letter from Mr. Anagnos with the comforting assurance that a teacher had been found. This was in the summer of 1886. But Miss Sullivan did not arrive until the following March.

Thus I came up out of Egypt and stood before Sinai, and a power divine touched my spirit and gave it sight, so that I beheld many wonders. And from the sacred mountain I heard a voice which said, "Knowledge is love and light and vision."

□

4

The most important day I remember in all my life is the one on which my teacher, Anne Mansfield Sullivan, came to me. I am filled with wonder when I consider the immeasurable contrasts between the two lives which it connects. It was the third of March, 1887, three months before I turned seven years old.

On the afternoon of that eventful day, I stood on the porch, dumb, expectant. I guessed vaguely from my mother's signs and from the hurrying to and fro in the house that something unusual was about to happen, so I went to the door and waited on the steps. The afternoon sun penetrated the mass of honeysuckle that covered the porch, and fell on my upturned face. My fingers lingered almost unconsciously on the familiar leaves and blossoms which had just come forth to greet the sweet southern spring. I did not know what the future held, of marvel or surprise for me. Anger and bitterness had preyed upon me continually for weeks and a deep languor had succeeded this passionate struggle.

Have you ever been at sea in a dense fog, when it seemed as if a tangible white darkness had shut you in, and the great ship, tense and anxious, groped her way towards the shore with plummet and sounding-line, and you waited with beating heart for something to happen? I was like that ship before my education began, only I was without compass or sounding-line, and had no way of knowing how near the harbour was. "Light! give me light!" was the wordless cry of my soul, and the light of love shone on me at that very hour.

I felt approaching footsteps, stretched out my hand as I supposed to my mother. Someone took it, and I was caught up and held close in the arms of her who had come to reveal all things to me, and, more than all things else, to love me.

The morning after my teacher came she led me into her room and gave me a doll. The little blind children at the Perkins Institution had sent it and Laura Bridgman had dressed it; but I did not know this until afterwards. When I had played with it a little while, Miss Sullivan slowly spelled into my hand the word "d-o-l-l."

The morning after my teacher came she led me into her room and gave me a doll. The little blind children at the Perkins Institution had sent it and Laura Bridgman had dressed it; but I did not know this until afterwards. When I had played with it a little while, Miss Sullivan slowly spelled into my hand the word "d-o-l-l." I was at once interested in this finger play and tried to imitate it. When I finally succeeded in making the letters correctly I was flushed with childish pleasure and pride. Running downstairs to my mother I held up my hand and made the letters for doll. I did not know that I was spelling a word or even that words existed; I was simply making my fingers go in monkey-like imitation. In the days that followed I learnt to spell a great many words in this uncomprehending way, like *pin, hat, cup* and a few verbs like *sit, stand* and *walk.* But my teacher had been with me for several weeks before I understood that everything had a name.

One day, while I was playing with my new doll, Miss Sullivan put my big rag doll also into my lap also, spelled "d-o-l-l" and tried to make me understand that "d-o-l-l" applied to both. Earlier in the day we had had a tussle over the words "m-u-g" and "w-a-t-e-r." Miss Sullivan had tried to impress it upon me that "m-u-g" is *mug* and that "w-a-t-e-r" is *water*, but I persisted in confounding the two. In despair she had dropped the subject for the time, only to renew it at the first opportunity. I became impatient at her repeated attempts and, seizing the new doll, I dashed it upon the floor. I was keenly delighted when I felt the fragments of the broken doll at my feet. Neither sorrow nor regret followed my passionate outburst. I had not loved the doll. In the still, dark world in which I lived there was no strong sentiment or tenderness. I felt my teacher sweep the fragments to one side of the hearth, and had a sense of satisfaction that the cause of my discomfort was removed. She brought me my hat, and I knew I was going out into the warm sunshine. This thought, if a wordless sensation may be called a thought, made me hop and skip with pleasure.

One day, while I was playing with my new doll, Miss Sullivan put my big rag doll also into my lap also, spelled "d-o-l-l" and tried to make me understand that "d-o-l-l" applied to both. Earlier in the day we had had a tussle over the words "m-u-g" and "w-a-t-e-r."

We walked down the path to the well-house, attracted by the fragrance of the honeysuckle with which it was covered. Someone was drawing water and my teacher placed my hand under the spout. As the cool stream gushed over one hand she spelled the word water into the other, first slowly, then rapidly. I stood still, my whole attention fixed upon the motions of her fingers. Suddenly I felt a misty consciousness as of something forgotten—a thrill of returning thought; and somehow the mystery of language was revealed to me. I knew then that "w-a-t-e-r" meant the wonderful cool something that was flowing over my hand. That living word awakened my soul, gave it light, hope, and joy and set it free! There were barriers still, it is true, but barriers that could in time be swept away.

I left the well-house eager to learn. Everything had a name, and each name gave birth to a new thought. As we returned to the house, every object which I touched seemed to quiver with life. That was because I saw everything with the strange, new sight that had come to me. On entering the door I remembered the doll that I had broken.

I left the well-house eager to learn. Everything had a name, and each name gave birth to a new thought. As we returned to the house, every object which I touched seemed to quiver with life. That was because I saw everything with the strange, new sight that had come to me. On entering the door I remembered the doll that I had broken. I felt my way to the hearth and picked up the pieces. I tried vainly to put them together. Then my eyes filled with tears; for I realised what I had done, and for the first time I felt repentance and sorrow.

I learnt a great many new words that day. I do not remember what they all were; but I do know that *mother, father, sister, teacher* were among them—words that were to make the world blossom for me, "like Aaron's rod, with flowers." It would have been difficult to find a happier child than I was as I lay in my crib at the close of that eventful day and lived over the joys it had brought me, and for the first time longed for a new day to come.

□

5

I recall many incidents of the summer of 1887 that followed my soul's sudden awakening. I did nothing but explore with my hands and learn the name of every object that I touched; and the more I handled things and learnt their names and uses, the more joyous and confident grew my sense of kinship with the rest of the world.

When the time of daisies and buttercups came, Miss Sullivan took me by the hand across the fields where men were preparing the earth for the seed, to the banks of the Tennessee River, and there, sitting on the warm grass, I had my first lessons in the beneficence of Nature. I learnt how the sun and the rain make every tree, that is pleasant to the sight and good for food, grow out of the ground, how birds build their nests and live and thrive from land to land, how the squirrel, the deer, the lion and every other creature finds food and shelter. As my knowledge of things grew, I was filled with delight about the world I was in. Long before I learnt to do a sum in arithmetic or describe the shape of the earth, Miss Sullivan had taught me to find beauty in the fragrant woods, in every blade of grass, and in the curves and dimples of my baby sister's hand. She linked my earliest thoughts with Nature, and made me feel that "birds and flowers and I were happy peers."

But about this time I had an experience which taught me that Nature is not always kind. One day my teacher and

I were returning from a long ramble. The morning had been fine, but it was growing warm and sultry when at last we turned our faces homewards. Two or three times we stopped to rest under a tree by the wayside. Our last halt was under a wild cherry tree, a short distance from the house. The shade made us grateful, and the tree was so easy to climb that with my teacher's assistance I was able to scramble to a seat in the branches. It was so cool up in the tree that Miss Sullivan proposed that we have our luncheon there. I promised to keep still while she went to the house to fetch it.

Suddenly a change passed over the tree. All the sun's warmth left the air. I knew the sky was black, because all the heat, which meant light to me, had died out of the atmosphere. A strange odour came up from the earth. I knew it, it was the odour that always precedes a thunderstorm, and a nameless fear clutched at my heart. I felt absolutely alone, cut off from my friends and the firm earth. The immense, the unknown, enfolded me. I remained still and expectant as a chilling terror crept over me. I longed for my teacher's return; but above all things I wanted to get down from that tree.

Suddenly a change passed over the tree. All the sun's warmth left the air. I knew the sky was black, because all the heat, which meant light to me, had died out of the atmosphere. A strange odour came up from the earth.

There was a moment of sinister silence, then a multitudinous stirring of the leaves. A shiver ran through the tree, and the wind sent forth a blast that would have knocked me off had I not clung to the branch with might and main. The tree swayed and strained. The small twigs snapped and fell about me in showers. A wild impulse to jump seized me, but terror held me fast. I crouched down in the fork of the tree. The branches lashed around me. I felt the intermittent jarring that came now and then, as if something heavy had fallen and the shock had travelled up till it reached the limb I sat on. It worked my suspense up to the highest point, and just as I was thinking that the tree and I would fall together, my teacher seized my hand and helped me down. I clung to her, trembling with joy to feel the earth under my feet once more. I had learnt a new lesson—that Nature "wages open war against her children, and under the softest touch hides treacherous claws."

After this experience it was a long time before I climbed another tree. The mere thought filled me with terror. It was the sweet allurement of the mimosa tree in full bloom that finally overcame my fears. One beautiful spring morning when I was alone in the summer-house, reading, I became aware of a wonderful subtle fragrance in the air. I started up and instinctively stretched out my hands. It seemed as if the spirit of spring had passed through the summer-house. "What is it?" I asked, and the next minute I recognised the odour of the mimosa blossoms. I felt my way to the end of the garden, knowing that the mimosa tree was near the fence, at the turn of the path. Yes, there it was, all quivering in the warm sunshine, its blossom-laden branches almost touching

After this experience it was a long time before I climbed another tree. The mere thought filled me with terror. It was the sweet allurement of the mimosa tree in full bloom that finally overcame my fears. One beautiful spring morning when I was alone in the summer-house, reading, I became aware of a wonderful subtle fragrance in the air.

the long grass. Was there ever anything so exquisitely beautiful in the world before? Its delicate blossoms shrank from the slightest earthly touch; it seemed as if a tree of paradise had been transplanted to earth. I made my way through a shower of petals to the great trunk and for one minute stood irresolute; then, putting my foot in the broad space between the forked branches, I pulled myself up into the tree. I had some difficulty in holding on, for the branches were very large and the bark hurt my hands. But I had a delicious sense that I was doing something unusual and wonderful so I kept on climbing higher and higher, until I reached a little seat which somebody had built there so long ago that it had become a part of the tree itself. I sat there for a long, long time, feeling like a fairy on a rosy cloud. After that I spent many happy hours in my tree of paradise, thinking fair thoughts and dreaming bright dreams.

□

6

I had now the key to all language, and I was eager to learn to use it. Children who can hear acquire language without any particular effort; they catch the words that fall from others' lips, by the wing, as it were, delightedly, while the little deaf child must trap them by a slow and often painful process. But whatever the process, the result is wonderful. Gradually from naming an object we advance step by step until we have traversed the vast distance between our first stammered syllable and the sweep of thought in a line of Shakespeare.

At first, when my teacher told me about a new thing I asked very few questions. My ideas were vague, and my vocabulary was inadequate; but as my knowledge of things grew, and I learnt more and more words, my field of inquiry broadened, and I would return again and again to the same subject, eager for further information. Sometimes a new word revived an image that some earlier experience had engraved on my brain.

I remember the morning that I first asked the meaning of the word, "love." This was before I knew many words. I had found a few early violets in the garden and brought them to my teacher. She tried to kiss me: but at that time I did not like to have anyone kiss me except my mother. Miss Sullivan put her arm gently round me and spelled into my hand, "I love Helen."

"What is love?" I asked.

She drew me closer to her and said, "It is here," pointing to my heart, whose beats I was conscious of for the first time. Her words puzzled me very much because I did not then understand anything unless I touched it.

I smelled the violets in her hand and asked, half in words, half in signs, a question which meant, "Is love the sweetness of flowers?"

"No," said my teacher.

Again I thought. The warm sun was shining on us.

"Is this not love?" I asked, pointing in the direction from which the heat came. "Is this not love?"

It seemed to me that there could be nothing more beautiful than the sun, whose warmth makes all things grow. But Miss Sullivan shook her head, and I was greatly puzzled and disappointed. I thought it strange that my teacher could not show me love.

It seemed to me that there could be nothing more beautiful than the sun, whose warmth makes all things grow. But Miss Sullivan shook her head, and I was greatly puzzled and disappointed. I thought it strange that my teacher could not show me love.

A day or two afterwards I was stringing beads of different sizes in symmetrical groups—two large beads, three small ones, and so on. I had made many mistakes, and Miss Sullivan had pointed them out again and again with gentle patience. Finally I noticed a very obvious error in the sequence and for an instant I concentrated my attention on the lesson and tried to think how I should have arranged the beads. Miss Sullivan touched my forehead and spelled with decided emphasis, "Think."

In a flash I knew that the word was the name of the process that was going on in my head. This was my first conscious perception of an abstract idea.

For a long time I was still—I was not thinking of the beads in my lap, but trying to find a meaning for "love" in the light of this new idea. The sun had been under a cloud all day, and there had been brief showers; but suddenly the sun broke forth in all its southern splendour.

"Love is something like the clouds that were in the sky before the sun came out," she replied. Then in simpler words than these, which at that time I could not have understood, she explained: "You cannot touch the clouds, you know; but you feel the rain and know how glad the flowers and the thirsty earth are to have it after a hot day."

Again I asked my teacher, "Is this not love?"

"Love is something like the clouds that were in the sky before the sun came out," she replied. Then in simpler words than these, which at that time I could not have understood, she explained: "You cannot touch the clouds, you know; but you feel the rain and know how glad the flowers and the thirsty earth are to have it after a hot day. You cannot touch love either; but you can feel the sweetness that it pours into everything. Without love you would not be happy or want to play."

The beautiful truth burst upon my mind—I felt that there were invisible lines stretched between my spirit and the spirits of others.

From the beginning of my education, Miss Sullivan made it a practice to speak to me as she would speak to any hearing child; the only difference was that she spelled the sentences into my hand instead of speaking them. If I did not know the words and idioms necessary to express my thoughts she supplied them, even suggesting conversation when I was unable to keep up my end of the dialogue.

This process was continued for several years; for the deaf child does not learn in a month or even in two or three years, the numberless idioms and expressions used in the simplest daily intercourse. The little hearing child learns these from constant repetition and imitation. The conversation he hears in his home stimulates his mind and suggests topics and calls forth the spontaneous expression of his own thoughts. This natural exchange of ideas is denied to the deaf child. My teacher, realising this, was determined to supply the kinds of stimulus I lacked. This she did by repeating to me as far as possible, verbatim, what she heard, and by showing me how I could take part in the conversation. But it was a long time before I ventured to take the initiative, and still longer before I could find something appropriate to say at the right time.

This process was continued for several years; for the deaf child does not learn in a month or even in two or three years, the numberless idioms and expressions used in the simplest daily intercourse. The little hearing child learns these from constant repetition and imitation.

The deaf or the blind find it very difficult to acquire the amenities of conversation. How much more this difficulty must be augmented in the case of those who are both deaf and blind! Without assistance, they cannot distinguish the tone of the voice or go up and down the gamut of tones that give significance to words; nor can they watch the expression of the speaker's face, and a look is often the very soul of what one says.

☐

7

The next important step in my education was learning to read. As soon as I could spell a few words, my teacher gave me slips of cardboard on which were printed words in raised letters. I quickly learnt that each printed word stood for an object, an act, or a quality. I had a frame in which I could arrange the words in little sentences; but before I ever put sentences in the frame I used to make them in objects. I found the slips of paper which represented, for example, "doll," "is," "on," "bed" and placed each name on its object; then I put my doll on the bed with the words *is, on, bed* arranged beside the doll, thus making a sentence of the words, and at the same time carrying out the idea of the sentence with the things themselves.

One day, Miss Sullivan tells me, I pinned the word *girl* on my pinafore and stood in the wardrobe. On the shelf I arranged the words, *is, in, wardrobe.* Nothing delighted me so much as this game. My teacher and I played it for hours at a time. Often everything in the room was arranged in object sentences.

From the printed slip it was but a step to the printed book. I took my "Reader for Beginners" and hunted for the words I knew and when I found them my joy was like that of a game of hide-and-seek. Thus I began to read. Of the time when I began to read connected stories, I shall speak later.

For a long time I had no regular lessons. Even when I studied most earnestly it seemed more like play than work. Miss Sullivan illustrated everything she taught me with a beautiful story or a poem. Whenever anything delighted or interested me, she talked it over with me just as if she were a little girl herself. What many children think of with dread, as a painful plodding through grammar, hard sums and harder definitions, is today one of my most precious memories.

I cannot explain the peculiar sympathy Miss Sullivan had with my pleasures and desires. Perhaps it was the result of her long association with the blind. Added to this she had a wonderful faculty for description. She went quickly over uninteresting details, and never nagged me with questions to see if I remembered the day-before-yesterday's lesson. She introduced dry technicalities of science little by little, making every subject so real that I could not help remembering what she taught.

I cannot explain the peculiar sympathy Miss Sullivan had with my pleasures and desires. Perhaps it was the result of her long association with the blind. Added to this she had a wonderful faculty for description. She went quickly over uninteresting details, and never nagged me with questions to see if I remembered the day-before-yesterday's lesson.

We read and studied out of doors, preferring the sunlit woods to the house. All my early lessons have in them the breath of the woods—the fine, resinous odour of pine needles, blended with the perfume of wild grapes. Seated in the gracious shade of a wild tulip tree, I learnt to think that everything has a lesson and a suggestion. "The loveliness of things taught me all their use." Indeed, everything that could hum, or buzz, or sing, or bloom had a part in my education; noisy-throated frogs, katydids and crickets held in my hand until forgetting their embarrassment, they trilled their reedy note, little downy chickens and wildflowers, the dogwood blossoms, meadow-violets and budding fruit trees. I felt the bursting cotton-bolls and fingered their soft fibre and fuzzy seeds; I felt the low whistling of the wind through the cornstalks, the silky rustling of the long leaves, and the indignant snort of my pony, as we caught him in the pasture and put the bit in his mouth—ah me! How well I remember the spicy, clovery smell of his breath!

Sometimes I rose at dawn and stole into the garden while the heavy dew lay on the grass and flowers. Few know the joy of feeling the roses pressing softly into the hand, or the beautiful motion of the lilies as they sway in the morning breeze. Sometimes I caught an insect in the flower I was plucking, and I felt the faint noise of a pair of wings rubbed together in a sudden terror, as the little creature became aware of a pressure from without.

Sometimes I rose at dawn and stole into the garden while the heavy dew lay on the grass and flowers. Few know the joy of feeling the roses pressing softly into the hand, or the beautiful motion of the lilies as they sway in the morning breeze.

Another favourite haunt of mine was the orchard where the fruit ripened early in July. The large, downy peaches would reach themselves into my hand, and the apples tumbled at my feet as the joyous breeze blew about the trees. Oh, the delight with which I gathered up the fruit in my pinafore and pressed my face against the smooth cheeks of the apples, still warm from the sun, and skipped back to the house!

Our favourite walk was to Keller's Landing, an old tumbledown lumber-wharf on the Tennessee River, used during the Civil War to land soldiers. There we spent many happy hours and played at learning geography. I built dams of pebbles, made islands and lakes, and dug river-beds, all for fun, and never dreamt that I was learning a lesson. I listened with increasing wonder to Miss Sullivan's descriptions of the great round world with its burning mountains, buried cities, moving rivers of ice, and many other things as strange. She made raised maps in clay so that I could feel the mountain ridges and valleys, and follow with my fingers the devious course of rivers. I liked this, too; but the division of the earth into zones and poles confused and teased my mind. The illustrative strings and the orange stick representing the poles seemed so real that even to this day the mere mention of temperate zone suggests a series of twine circles; and I believe that if anyone should set about it he could convince me that white bears actually climb the North Pole.

Our favourite walk was to Keller's Landing, an old tumbledown lumber-wharf on the Tennessee River, used during the Civil War to land soldiers. There we spent many happy hours and played at learning geography. I built dams of pebbles, made islands and lakes, and dug river-beds, all for fun, and never dreamt that I was learning a lesson.

Arithmetic seems to have been the only study I did not

like. From the first I was not interested in the science of numbers. Miss Sullivan tried to teach me to count by stringing beads in groups, and I learnt to add and subtract by arranging kindergarten straws. I never had the patience to arrange more than five or six groups at a time. When I had accomplished this my conscience was at rest for the day, and I went out quickly to find my playmates.

In this same leisurely manner I studied zoology and botany.

Once a gentleman, whose name I have forgotten, sent me a collection of fossils—tiny mollusc shells beautifully marked, and bits of sandstone with the print of birds' claws, and a lovely fern in bas-relief. These were the keys which unlocked the treasures of the antediluvian world for me. With trembling fingers I listened to Miss Sullivan's descriptions of the terrible beasts, with uncouth, unpronounceable names, which once went tramping through the primeval forests, tearing down the branches of gigantic trees for food, and died in the dismal swamps of an unknown age. For a long time these strange creatures haunted my dreams, and this gloomy period formed a sombre background to the joyous world now, filled with sunshine and roses and echoing with the gentle beat of my pony's hoof.

Once a gentleman, whose name I have forgotten, sent me a collection of fossils—tiny mollusc shells beautifully marked, and bits of sandstone with the print of birds' claws, and a lovely fern in bas-relief. These were the keys which unlocked the treasures of the antediluvian world for me.

Another time a beautiful shell was given me, and with a child's surprise and delight I learnt how a tiny mollusc had built the lustrous coil for his dwelling place, and how on still nights, when there is no breeze stirring the waves, the Nautilus sails on the blue waters of the Indian Ocean in his "ship of pearl." After I had learnt a great many interesting things about the life and habits of the children of the sea—how in the midst of dashing waves the little polyps build the beautiful coral isles of the Pacific, and the foraminifera have made the chalk-hills of many a land—my teacher read me "The Chambered Nautilus," and showed me that the shell-building process of the molluscs is symbolic of the development of the mind. Just as the wonder-working mantle of the Nautilus changes the material it absorbs from the water and makes it a part of itself, so also the bits of knowledge one gathers undergo a similar change and become pearls of thought.

Again, it was the growth of a plant that furnished the text for a lesson. We bought a lily and set it in a sunny window. Very soon the green, pointed buds showed signs of opening. The slender, fingerlike leaves on the outside opened slowly, reluctant, I thought, to reveal the loveliness they hid.

Again, it was the growth of a plant that furnished the text for a lesson. We bought a lily and set it in a sunny window. Very soon the green, pointed buds showed signs of opening. The slender, fingerlike leaves on the outside opened slowly, reluctant, I thought, to reveal the loveliness they hid. Once having made a start, however, the opening process went on rapidly, but in order and systematically. There was always one bud larger and more beautiful than the rest, which pushed her outer, covering back with more pomp, as if the beauty in soft, silky robes knew that she was the lily-queen by right divine, while her more timid sisters doffed their green hoods shyly, until the whole plant was one nodding bough of loveliness and fragrance.

Once there were eleven tadpoles in a glass globe set in a window full of plants. I remember the eagerness with which I made discoveries about them. It was great fun to plunge my hand into the bowl and feel the tadpoles frisk about, and to let them slip and slide between my fingers. One day, a more ambitious fellow leaped beyond the edge of the bowl and fell on the floor, where I found him to all appearance more dead than alive. The only sign of life was a slight wriggling of his tail. But no sooner had he returned to his element than he darted to the bottom, swimming round and round in joyous activity. He had made his leap, he had seen the great world, and was content to stay in his pretty glass house under the big fuchsia tree until he attained the dignity of frog hood. Then he went to live in the leafy pool at the end of the garden, where he made the summer nights musical with his quaint love-song.

Once there were eleven tadpoles in a glass globe set in a window full of plants. I remember the eagerness with which I made discoveries about them. It was great fun to plunge my hand into the bowl and feel the tadpoles frisk about, and to let them slip and slide between my fingers.

Thus I learnt from life itself. At the beginning I was only a little mass of possibilities. It was my teacher who unfolded and developed them. After she came, everything about me breathed of love and joy and was full of meaning. She has never since let pass an opportunity to point out the beauty that is in everything, nor has she ceased trying in thought and action and example to make my life sweet and useful.

It was my teacher's genius, her quick sympathy, her loving tact which made the first years of my education so beautiful. It was because she seized the right moment to impart knowledge that made it so pleasant and acceptable to me. She realised that a child's mind is like a shallow brook which ripples and dances merrily over the stony course of its education and reflects here a flower, there a bush, yonder a fleecy cloud; and she attempted to guide my mind on its way, knowing that like a brook it should be fed by mountain streams and hidden springs, until it broadened out into a deep river, capable of reflecting in its placid surface, billowy hills, the luminous shadows of trees and the blue heavens, as well as the sweet face of a little flower.

My teacher is so near to me that I scarcely think of myself apart from her. How much of my delight in all beautiful things is innate, and how much is due to her influence, I can never tell. I feel that her being is inseparable from my own, and that the footsteps of my life are in hers.

Any teacher can take a child to the classroom, but not every teacher can make him learn. He will not work joyously unless he feels that liberty is his, whether he is busy or at rest; he must feel the flush of victory and the heart-sinking of disappointment before he willingly takes up the tasks distasteful to him and resolves to dance his way bravely through a dull routine of textbooks.

My teacher is so near to me that I scarcely think of myself apart from her. How much of my delight in all beautiful things is innate, and how much is due to her influence, I can never tell. I feel that her being is inseparable from my own, and that the footsteps of my life are in hers. All the best of me belongs to her—there is not a talent, or an aspiration or a joy in me that has not been awakened by her loving touch.

□

8

The first Christmas after Miss Sullivan came to Tuscumbia was a great event. Everyone in the family prepared surprises for me, but what pleased me most were the surprises that Miss Sullivan and I prepared for everybody else. The mystery that surrounded the gifts was my greatest delight and amusement. My friends did all they could to excite my curiosity by hints and half-spelled sentences which they pretended to break off in the nick of time. Miss Sullivan and I kept up a game of guessing which taught me more about the use of language than any set lessons could have done. Every evening, seated round a glowing wood fire, we played our guessing game, which grew more and more exciting as Christmas approached.

On Christmas Eve the Tuscumbia schoolchildren had their tree, to which they invited me. In the centre of the schoolroom stood a beautiful tree ablaze and shimmering in the soft light, its branches loaded with strange, wonderful fruit. It was a moment of supreme happiness. I danced and capered round the tree in ecstasy. When I learnt that there was a gift for each child, I was delighted, and the kind people who had prepared the tree permitted me to hand the presents to the children. In the pleasure of doing this, I did not stop to look at my own gifts; but when I was ready for them, my impatience for the real Christmas to begin almost got beyond control. I knew the gifts I already had were not those of which friends had thrown out such tantalising hints, and my teacher said the presents I was to have would be even nicer than these. I was persuaded, however, to content myself with the gifts from the tree and leave the others until morning.

That night, after I had hung my stocking, I lay awake for a long time, pretending to be asleep and keeping alert to see what Santa Claus would do when he came. At last I fell asleep with a new doll and a white bear in my arms. Next morning it was I who woke the whole family with my first "Merry Christmas!" I found surprises, not in the stocking only, but on the table, on all the chairs, at the door, on the very window-sill; indeed, I could hardly walk without stumbling on a bit of Christmas wrapped up in tissue paper. But when my teacher presented me with a canary, my cup of happiness overflowed.

That night, after I had hung my stocking, I lay awake for a long time, pretending to be asleep and keeping alert to see what Santa Claus would do when he came. At last I fell asleep with a new doll and a white bear in my arms. Next morning it was I who woke the whole family with my first "Merry Christmas!"

Little Tim was so tame that he would hop on my finger and eat candied cherries out of my hand. Miss Sullivan taught me to take care of my new pet. Every morning after breakfast I prepared his bath, made his cage clean and sweet, filled his cups with fresh seed and water from the well-house, and hung a spray of chickweed in his swing.

One morning I left the cage on the window-seat while I went to fetch water for his bath. When I returned I felt a big cat brush past me as I opened the door. At first I did not realise what had happened; but when I put my hand in the cage and Tim's pretty wings did not meet my touch or his small pointed claws did not take hold of my finger, I knew that I would never see my sweet little singer again.

□

9

The next important event in my life was my visit to Boston, in May, 1888. I remember the preparations as if it were yesterday. I can vividly recollect the departure with my teacher and my mother, the journey, and finally the arrival in Boston. How different this journey was from the one I had made to Baltimore two years before! I was no longer a restless, excitable little creature, requiring the attention of everybody on the train to keep me amused. I sat quietly beside Miss Sullivan, taking in with eager interest all that she told me about what she saw out of the car window: the beautiful Tennessee River, the great cotton-fields, the hills and woods, and the crowds of laughing Negroes at the stations, who waved to the people on the train and brought delicious candy and popcorn balls through the car. On the seat opposite me sat my big rag doll, Nancy, in a new gingham dress and a ruffled sunbonnet, looking at me out of two bead eyes. Sometimes, when I was not absorbed in Miss Sullivan's descriptions, I remembered Nancy's existence and took her up in my arms, but I generally calmed my conscience by making myself believe that she was asleep.

As I shall not have occasion to refer to Nancy again, I wish to tell here a sad experience she had soon after our arrival in Boston. She was covered with dirt—the remains of mud pies I had compelled her to eat, although she had never shown any special liking for them. The laundress at the Perkins Institution secretly carried her off to give her a bath. This was too much for poor Nancy. When I next saw her she was a formless heap of cotton, which I should not have recognised at all except for the two bead eyes which looked out at me reproachfully.

When the train at last pulled into the station at Boston it was as if a beautiful fairy tale had come true. The "once upon a time" was now; the "far-away country" was here.

We had scarcely arrived at the Perkins Institution for the Blind when I began to make friends with the little blind children. It delighted me inexpressibly to find that they knew the manual alphabet. What joy to talk with other children in my own language! Until then I had been like a foreigner speaking through an interpreter. In the school where Laura Bridgman was taught, I was in my own country. It took me some time to appreciate the fact that my new friends were blind. I knew I could not see; but it did not seem possible that all the eager, loving children who gathered round me and joined heartily in my frolics were also blind. I remember the surprise and the pain I felt as I noticed that they placed their hands over mine when I talked to them and that they read books with their fingers. Although I had been told this before, and although I understood my own deprivations, yet I had thought vaguely that since they could hear, they must have a sort of "second sight," and I was not prepared to find one child and another and yet another deprived of the same precious gift. But they were so happy and contented that I

When the train at last pulled into the station at Boston it was as if a beautiful fairy tale had come true. The "once upon a time" was now; the "far-away country" was here.

lost all sense of pain in the pleasure of their companionship.

One day spent with the blind children made me feel thoroughly at home in my new environment, and I looked eagerly from one pleasant experience to another as the days flew swiftly by. I could not quite convince myself that there was much world left, for I regarded Boston as the beginning and the end of creation.

One day spent with the blind children made me feel thoroughly at home in my new environment, and I looked eagerly from one pleasant experience to another as the days flew swiftly by. I could not quite convince myself that there was much world left, for I regarded Boston as the beginning and the end of creation.

While we were in Boston we visited Bunker Hill, and there I had my first lesson in history. The story of the brave men who had fought on the spot where we stood excited me greatly. I climbed the monument, counting the steps, and wondering as I went higher and yet higher if the soldiers had climbed this great stairway and shot at the enemy on the ground below.

The next day we went to Plymouth by water. This was my first trip on the ocean and my first voyage in a steamboat. How full of life and motion it was! But the rumble of the machinery made me think it was thundering, and I began to cry, because I feared that if it rained we would not be able to have our picnic out of doors. I was more interested, I think, in the great rock on which the Pilgrims landed than in anything else in Plymouth. I could touch it, and perhaps that made the coming of the Pilgrims and their toils and great deeds seem more real to me. I had often held in my hand a little model of the

Plymouth Rock which a kind gentleman had given me at Pilgrim Hall, and I had fingered its curves, the split in the centre and the embossed figures "1620," and turned over in my mind all that I knew about the wonderful story of the Pilgrims.

How my childish imagination glowed with the splendour of their enterprise! I idealised them as the bravest and most generous men that ever sought a home in a strange land. I thought they desired the freedom of their fellow men as well as their own. I was keenly surprised and disappointed years later to learn of their acts of persecution that make us tingle with shame, even while we honour the courage and energy that gave us our "Country Beautiful."

How my childish imagination glowed with the splendour of their enterprise! I idealised them as the bravest and most generous men that ever sought a home in a strange land. I thought they desired the freedom of their fellow men as well as their own.

Among the many friends I made in Boston were Mr. William Endicott and his daughter. Their kindness to me was the seed from which many pleasant memories have since grown. One day we visited their beautiful home at Beverly Farms. I remember with delight how I went through their rose-garden, how their dogs, big Leo and little curly-haired Fritz with long ears, came to meet me, and how Nimrod, the swiftest of the horses, poked his nose into my hands for a pat and a lump of sugar. I also remember the beach, where for the first time I had played in the sand. It was hard, smooth sand, very different from the loose, sharp sand, mingled with kelp and shells, at Brewster. Mr.

Endicott told me about the great ships that came sailing by from Boston, bound for Europe. I saw him many times after that, and he was always a good friend to me. I was indeed thinking of him when I called Boston "the City of Kind Hearts."

□

10

Just before the Perkins Institution closed for the summer, it was arranged that my teacher and I should spend our vacation at Brewster, on Cape Cod, with our dear friend, Mrs. Hopkins. I was delighted, for my mind was full of the prospective joys and of the wonderful stories I had heard about the sea.

My most vivid recollection of that summer is the ocean. I had always lived far inland and had never had so much as a whiff of salt air; but I had read in a big book called "Our World" a description of the ocean which filled me with wonder and an intense longing to touch the mighty sea and feel it roar. So my little heart leaped high with eager excitement when I knew that my wish was at last to realised.

No sooner had I been helped into my bathing-suit than I sprang out upon the warm sand and without a thought of fear plunged into the cool water. I felt the great billows rock and sink. The buoyant motion of the water filled me with an exquisite, quivering joy. Suddenly my ecstasy gave place to terror; for my foot struck against a rock and the next instant there was a rush of water over my head. I thrust out my hands to grasp some support, I clutched at the water and at the seaweed which the waves tossed in my face. But all my frantic efforts were in vain. The waves seemed to be playing a game with me, and tossed me from one to another in their wild frolic. It was fearful! The good, firm earth had slipped from my feet, and everything seemed shut out from this strange, all-enveloping element—life, air, warmth and love. At last, however, the sea, as if weary of its new toy, threw me back on the shore, and in another instant I was clasped in my teacher's arms. Oh, the comfort of the long, tender embrace! As soon as I had recovered from my panic sufficiently to say anything, I demanded: "Who put salt in the water?"

After I had recovered from my first experience in the water, I thought it great fun to sit on a big rock in my bathing-suit and feel wave after wave dash against the rock, sending up a shower of spray which quite covered me. I felt the pebbles rattling as the waves threw their ponderous weight against the shore. The whole beach seemed racked by their terrific onset and the air throbbed with their pulsations. The breakers would swoop back to gather themselves for a mightier leap, and I clung to the rock, tense, fascinated, as I felt the dash and roar of the rushing sea!

After I had recovered from my first experience in the water, I thought it great fun to sit on a big rock in my bathing-suit and fecl wave after wave dash against the rock, sending up a shower of spray which quite covered me. I felt the pebbles rattling as the waves threw their ponderous weight against the shore.

I could never stay long enough on the shore. The tang of the untainted, fresh and free sea air was like a cool, quieting thought, and I never lost fascination for the shells and pebbles and the seaweed with tiny living creatures attached to it. One day Miss Sullivan attracted my attention to a strange object which she had captured basking in the shallow water. It was a great horseshoe crab—the first one I had ever seen. I felt him and thought it very strange that he should carry his house on his back. It suddenly occurred to me that he might make a delightful pet; so I seized him by the tail with both hands and carried him home. This feat pleased me highly, as his body was very heavy, and it took all my strength to drag him half a mile. I would not leave Miss Sullivan in peace until she had put the crab in a trough near the well where I was confident he would be secure. But next morning I went to the trough, and lo, he had disappeared! Nobody knew where he had gone, or how he had escaped. My disappointment was bitter at the time; but little by little I came to realise that it had not been kind or wise of me to force this poor dumb creature out of his element, and after a while I felt happy in the thought that perhaps he had returned to the sea.

My disappointment was bitter at the time; but little by little I came to realise that it had not been kind or wise of me to force this poor dumb creature out of his element, and after a while I felt happy in the thought that perhaps he had returned to the sea.

11

In the autumn I returned to my Southern home with a heart full of joyous memories. As I recall that visit North, I am filled with wonder at the richness and variety of the experiences that cluster about it. It seems to have been the beginning of everything. The treasures of a new, beautiful world were laid at my feet, and I took in pleasure and information at every turn. I lived myself into all things. I was never still for a moment; my life was as full of motion as those little insects that crowd a whole existence into one brief day. I met many people who talked with me by spelling into my hand, and thought in joyous sympathy leaped up to meet thought, and behold, a miracle had been wrought! The barren places between my mind and the minds of others blossomed like the rose.

I spent the autumn months with my family at our summer cottage on a mountain about fourteen miles from Tuscumbia. It was called Fern Quarry, because near it there was a limestone quarry, long since abandoned. Three frolicsome little streams ran through it from springs in the rocks above, leaping here and tumbling there in laughing cascades wherever the rocks tried to bar their way. The opening was filled with ferns which completely covered the beds of limestone and in places hid the streams. The rest of the mountain was thickly wooded. There were great oaks and splendid evergreens with trunks like mossy pillars, from the branches of which hung garlands of ivy and mistletoe, and persimmon trees, the odour of which pervaded every nook and corner of the wood—an illusive, fragrant something that made the heart glad. In places the wild muscadine and scuppernong vines stretched from tree to tree, making arbours which were always full of butterflies and buzzing insects. It was delightful to lose ourselves in the green hollows of that tangled wood in the late afternoon, and to smell the cool, delicious odours that came up from the earth at the close of day.

> ***Our cottage was a sort of rough camp, beautifully situated on the top of the mountain among oaks and pines. The small rooms were arranged on each side of a long open hall. Around the house was a wide piazza, where the mountain winds blew, sweet with all wood-scents. We lived on the piazza most of the time—there we worked, ate and played.***

Our cottage was a sort of rough camp, beautifully situated on the top of the mountain among oaks and pines. The small rooms were arranged on each side of a long open hall. Around the house was a wide piazza, where the mountain winds blew, sweet with all wood-scents. We lived on the piazza most of the time—there we worked, ate and played. At the back door there was a great butternut tree, around which the steps had been built, and in front the trees stood so close that I could touch them and feel the wind shake their branches, or the leaves twirl downwards in the autumn blast.

Many visitors came to Fern Quarry. In the evening, the men played cards by the campfire and whiled away the hours in talk and sport. They told stories of their wonderful feats with fowl, fish and quadruped—how many wild ducks and turkeys they had shot, what "savage trout" they had caught, and how they had bagged the craftiest foxes, outwitted the most clever opossums and overtaken the fleetest deer, until I thought that surely the lion, the tiger, the bear and the rest of the wild tribe would not be able to stand before these wily hunters. "Tomorrow to the chase!" was their good-night shout as the circle of merry friends broke up for the night. The men slept in the hall outside our door, and I could feel the deep breathing of the dogs and the hunters as they lay on their improvised beds.

At dawn I was awakened by the smell of coffee, the rattling of guns, and the heavy footsteps of the men as they strode about, promising themselves the greatest luck of the season. I could also feel the stamping of the horses, which they had ridden out from town and hitched under the trees, where they stood all night, neighing loudly, impatient to be off. At last the men mounted, and, as they say in the old songs, away went the steeds with bridles ringing and whips cracking and hounds racing ahead, and away went the champion hunters "with hark and whoop and wild halloo!"

At dawn I was awakened by the smell of coffee, the rattling of guns, and the heavy footsteps of the men as they strode about, promising themselves the greatest luck of the season. I could also feel the stamping of the horses, which they had ridden out from town and hitched under the trees, where they stood all night, neighing loudly, impatient to be off.

Later in the morning we made preparations for a barbecue. A fire was kindled at the bottom of a deep hole in the ground, big sticks were laid crosswise at the top, and meat was hung from them and turned on spits. Around the fire squatted Negroes, driving away the flies with long branches. The savory odour of the meat made me hungry long before the tables were set.

When the bustle and excitement of preparation was at its height, the hunting party made its appearance, struggling in by twos and threes, the men hot and weary, the horses covered with foam, and the jaded hounds panting and dejected—and not a single kill! Every man declared that he had seen at least one deer and that the animal had come very close; but however hotly the dogs might pursue the game, however well the guns might be aimed, at the snap of the trigger there was not a deer in sight. They had been as fortunate as the little boy who said he came very near seeing a rabbit—he saw his tracks. The party soon forgot its disappointment, however, and we sat down, not to venison, but to a tamer feast of veal and roasted pig.

One summer I had my pony at Fern Quarry. I called him Black Beauty, as I had just read the book, and he resembled his namesake in every way, from his glossy black coat to the white star on his forehead. I spent many of my happiest hours on his back.

One summer I had my pony at Fern Quarry. I called him Black Beauty, as I had just read the book, and he resembled his namesake in every way, from his glossy black coat to the white star on his forehead. I spent many of my happiest hours on his back. Occasionally, when it was quite safe, my teacher would let go the leading-rein, and the pony sauntered on or stopped at his sweet will to eat grass or nibble at the leaves of the trees that grew beside the narrow trail.

On mornings when I did not care for the ride, my teacher and I would start after breakfast for a ramble in the woods, and allow ourselves to get lost amid the trees and vines, with no road to follow except the paths made by cows and horses. Frequently we came upon impassable thickets which forced us to take a round about way. We always returned to the cottage with armfuls of laurel, goldenrod, ferns and gorgeous swamp-flowers that grow only in the South.

Sometimes I would go with Mildred and my little cousins to gather persimmons. I did not eat them; but I loved their fragrance and enjoyed hunting for them in the leaves and grass. We also went nutting and I helped them open the chestnut burrs and break the shells of hickory-nuts and walnuts—the big, sweet walnuts!

Sometimes I would go with Mildred and my little cousins to gather persimmons. I did not eat them; but I loved their fragrance and enjoyed hunting for them in the leaves and grass. We also went nutting and I helped them open the chestnut burrs and break the shells of hickory-nuts and walnuts—the big, sweet walnuts!

At the foot of the mountain there was a railroad, and the children watched the trains as they whizzed by. Sometimes a terrific whistle brought us to the steps, and Mildred told me in great excitement that a cow or a horse had strayed on the track. At about a mile's distance there was a trestle spanning a deep gorge. It was very difficult to walk over; the ties were wide apart and so narrow that one felt as if one were walking on knives. I had never crossed it until one day Mildred, Miss Sullivan and I were lost in the woods, and wandered for hours without finding a path.

Suddenly Mildred pointed with her little hand and exclaimed, "There's the trestle!" We would have taken any way rather than that; but it was late and growing dark, and the trestle was a short cut home. I had to feel for the rails with my toe; but I was not afraid, and got on very well, until all at once there came a faint "puff, puff" from the distance.

"I see the train!" cried Mildred, and in another minute it would have been upon us had we not climbed down on the cross braces while it rushed over our heads. I felt the hot breath from the engine on my face, and the smoke and ashes almost choked us. As the train rumbled by, the trestle shook and swayed until I thought we should be dashed to the chasm below. With utmost difficulty we regained the track. Long after dark we reached home and found the cottage empty; the family were all out hunting for us.

□

12

After my first visit to Boston, I spent almost every winter in the North. Once I went on a visit to a New England village with its frozen lakes and vast snowfields. It was then that I had opportunities such as had never been mine to enter into the treasures of the snow.

I recall my surprise on discovering that a mysterious hand had stripped the trees and bushes, leaving only a wrinkled leaf here and there. The birds had flown away, and their empty nests in the bare trees were filled with snow. Winter was everywhere on the hill and the fields. The earth seemed benumbed by his icy touch, and the very spirits of the trees had withdrawn to their roots, and lay there fast asleep, curled up in the dark. All life seemed to have ebbed away, and even when the sun shone the day was Shrunk and Cold. As if her veins were sapless and old. And she rose up decrepitly for a last dim look at earth and sea.

The withered grass and the bushes were transformed into a forest of icicles.

Then came a day when the chilled air portended a snowstorm. We rushed out of doors to feel the first few tiny flakes descending. Hour by hour the flakes dropped silently, softly from their airy height to the earth, and the country became more and more level. A snowy night closed upon the world, and in the morning one could scarcely recognise a feature of the landscape. All the roads were hidden, not a single landmark was visible, only a waste of snow with trees rising out of it.

In the evening a wind from the northeast sprang up, and the flakes rushed hither and thither in furious melee. We sat around the great fire and told merry tales, and frolicked, and quite forgot that we were in the midst of a desolate solitude, shut in from all communication with the outside world. But during the night the fury of the wind increased to such a degree that it thrilled us with a vague terror. The rafters creaked and strained, and the branches of the trees surrounding the house rattled and beat against the windows, as the winds rioted up and down the country.

In the evening a wind from the northeast sprang up, and the flakes rushed hither and thither in furious melee. We sat around the great fire and told merry tales, and frolicked, and quite forgot that we were in the midst of a desolate solitude, shut in from all communication with the outside world.

On the third day after the beginning of the storm the snow ceased. The sun broke through the clouds and shone upon a vast, undulating white plain. High mounds, pyramids heaped in fantastic shapes, and impenetrable drifts lay scattered in every direction.

Narrow paths were shovelled through the drifts. I put on my cloak and hood and went out. The air stung my cheeks like fire. Half walking in the paths, half working our way through the lesser drifts, we succeeded in reaching a pine grove just outside a broad pasture. The trees stood motionless and white like figures in a marble frieze. There was no odour of pine needles. The rays of the sun fell upon the trees, and the twigs sparkled like diamonds and dropped in showers when we touched them. So dazzling was the light, it penetrated even the darkness that veils my eyes.

As the days wore on, the drifts gradually shrunk, but before they were wholly gone another storm came, so that I scarcely felt the earth under my feet even once all winter. At intervals the trees lost their icy covering, and the bulrushes and underbrush were bare; but the lake lay frozen and hard beneath the sun.

As the days wore on, the drifts gradually shrunk, but before they were wholly gone another storm came, so that I scarcely felt the earth under my feet even once all winter. At intervals the trees lost their icy covering, and the bulrushes and underbrush were bare; but the lake lay frozen and hard beneath the sun.

Our favourite amusement during that winter was tobogganing. In places the shore of the lake rises abruptly from the water's edge. Down these steep slopes we used to coast. We would get on our toboggan, a boy would give us a shove, and off we went! Plunging through drifts, leaping hollows, swooping down upon the lake, we would shoot across its gleaming surface to the opposite bank. What joy! What exhilarating madness! For one wild, glad moment we snapped the chain that binds us to earth, and joining hands with the winds we felt ourselves divine!

□

13

It was in the spring of 1890 that I learnt to speak. The impulse to utter audible sounds had always been strong within me. I used to make noises, keeping one hand on my throat while the other hand felt the movements of my lips. I was pleased with anything that made a noise and liked to feel the cat purr and the dog bark. I also liked to keep my hand on a singer's throat, or on a piano when it was being played. Before I lost my sight and hearing, I was fast learning to talk, but after my illness it was found that I had ceased to speak because I could not hear. I used to sit in my mother's lap all day long and keep my hands on her face because it amused me to feel the motions of her lips; and I moved my lips, too, although I had forgotten what talking was. My friends say that I laughed and cried naturally, and for a while I made many sounds and word-elements, not because they were a means of communication, but because the need of exercising my vocal organs was imperative. There was, however, one word the meaning of which I still remembered, WATER. I pronounced it as "wa-wa." Even this became less and less intelligible until the time when Miss Sullivan began to teach me. I stopped using it only after I had learnt to spell the word on my fingers.

I had known for a long time that the people around me used a method of communication different from mine; and even before I knew that a deaf child could be taught to speak, I was conscious of dissatisfaction with the means of communication I already possessed. One who is entirely dependent upon the manual alphabet has always a sense of restraint, of narrowness. This feeling began to agitate me with a vexing, forward-reaching sense of a lack that should be filled. My thoughts would often rise and beat up like birds against the wind, and I persisted in using my lips and voice. Friends tried to discourage this tendency, fearing lest it would lead to disappointment. But I persisted, and an accident soon occurred which resulted in the breaking down of this great barrier—I heard the story of Ragnhild Kaata.

In 1890 Mrs. Lamson, who had been one of Laura Bridgman's teachers, and who had just returned from a visit to Norway and Sweden, came to see me, and told me of Ragnhild Kaata, a deaf and blind girl in Norway who had actually been taught to speak. Mrs. Lamson had scarcely finished telling me about this girl's success when I was on fire with eagerness. I resolved that I, too, would learn to speak. I would not rest satisfied until my teacher took me, for advice and assistance, to Miss Sarah Fuller, principal of the Horace Mann School. This lovely, sweet-natured lady offered to teach me herself, and we began on the twenty-sixth of March 1890.

In 1890 Mrs. Lamson, who had been one of Laura Bridgman's teachers, and who had just returned from a visit to Norway and Sweden, came to see me, and told me of Ragnhild Kaata, a deaf and blind girl in Norway who had actually been taught to speak.

Miss Fuller's method was this: she passed my hand lightly over her face, and let me feel the position of her tongue and lips when she made a sound. I was eager to imitate every motion and in an hour had learnt six elements of speech: *M, P, A, S, T, I.* Miss Fuller gave me eleven lessons in all. I shall never forget the surprise and delight I felt when I uttered my first connected sentence, "It is warm." True, they were broken and stammering syllables; but they were human speech. My soul, conscious of new strength, came out of bondage, and was reaching through those broken symbols of speech to all knowledge and all faith.

No deaf child who has earnestly tried to speak the words which he has never heard—to come out of the prison of silence, where no tone of love, no song of bird, no strain of music ever pierces the stillness—can forget the thrill of surprise, the joy of discovery which came over him when he uttered his first word. Only such a one can appreciate the eagerness with which I talked to my toys, to stones, trees, birds and dumb animals, or the delight I felt when at my call Mildred ran to me or my dogs obeyed my commands. It is an unspeakable boon to me to be able to speak in winged words that need no interpretation. As I talked, happy thoughts fluttered up out of my words that might perhaps have struggled in vain to escape my fingers.

No deaf child who has earnestly tried to speak the words which he has never heard—to come out of the prison of silence, where no tone of love, no song of bird, no strain of music ever pierces the stillness—can forget the thrill of surprise, the joy of discovery which came over him when he uttered his first word.

But it must not be supposed that I could really talk in this short time. I had learnt only the elements of speech. Miss Fuller and Miss Sullivan could understand me, but most people would not have understood one word in a hundred. Nor is it true that, after I had learned these elements, I did the rest of the work myself. But for Miss Sullivan's genius, untiring perseverance and devotion, I could not have progressed as far as I have towards natural speech. In the first place, I laboured night and day before even my most intimate friends could understand me. In the second place, I needed Miss Sullivan's assistance constantly in my efforts to articulate each sound clearly and to combine all sounds in a thousand ways. Even now she calls my attention every day to mispronounced words.

All teachers of the deaf know what this means, and only they can appreciate the peculiar difficulties with which I had to contend. In reading my teacher's lips I was wholly dependent on my fingers: I had to use the sense of touch in catching the vibrations of the throat, the movements of the mouth and the expressions of the face; and often this sense was at fault.

All teachers of the deaf know what this means, and only they can appreciate the peculiar difficulties with which I had to contend. In reading my teacher's lips I was wholly dependent on my fingers: I had to use the sense of touch in catching the vibrations of the throat, the movements of the mouth and the expressions of the face; and often this sense was at fault. In such cases I was forced to repeat the words or sentences, sometimes for hours, until I felt the proper ring in my own voice. My work was practice, practice and more practice. Discouragement and weariness cast me down frequently; but the next moment the thought that I should soon be at home and show my loved ones what I had accomplished, spurred me on, and I eagerly looked forward to their pleasure in my achievement.

"My little sister will understand me now," was a thought stronger than all obstacles. I used to repeat ecstatically, "I am not dumb now." I could not be despondent while I anticipated the delight of talking to my mother and reading her responses from her lips. It astonished me to find how much easier it was to talk than to spell with the fingers, and I discarded the manual alphabet as a medium of communication on my part; but Miss Sullivan and a few friends still use it in speaking to me, for it is more convenient and more rapid than lip-reading.

"My little sister will understand me now," was a thought stronger than all obstacles. I used to repeat ecstatically, "I am not dumb now." I could not be despondent while I anticipated the delight of talking to my mother and reading her responses from her lips.

Just here, perhaps, I had better explain our use of the manual alphabet, which seems to puzzle people who do not know us. One who reads or talks to me spells with his hand, using the single-hand manual alphabet generally employed by the deaf. I place my hand on the hand of the speaker so lightly as not to impede its movements. The position of the hand is as easy to feel, as it is to see. I do not feel each letter any more than you see each letter separately when you read. Constant practice makes the fingers very flexible, and some of my friends spell rapidly—about as fast as an expert writes on a typewriter. The mere spelling is, of course, no more a conscious act than it is in writing.

When I had made speech my own, I could not wait to

go home. Finally, the happiest of all happy moments arrived. I had made my homeward journey, talking constantly to Miss Sullivan, not for the sake of talking, but determined to improve to the last minute. Almost before I knew it, the train stopped at the Tuscumbia station, and there on the platform stood the whole family. My eyes fill with tears now as I think how my mother pressed me close to her, speechless and trembling with delight, taking in every syllable that I spoke, while little Mildred seized my free hand and kissed it and danced, and my father expressed his pride and affection in a big silence. It was as if Isaiah's prophecy had been fulfilled in me, "The mountains and the hills shall break forth before you into singing, and all the trees of the field shall clap their hands!"

□

14

The winter of 1892 was darkened by the one dark cloud in my childhood's bright sky. Joy deserted my heart, and for a long, long time I lived in doubt, anxiety and fear. Books lost their charm for me, and even now the thought of those dreadful days chills my heart. A little story called "The Frost King," which I wrote and sent to Mr. Anagnos, of the Perkins Institution for the Blind, was at the root of the trouble. In order to make the matter clear, I must set forth the facts connected with this episode, which justice to my teacher and to myself compels me to relate.

I wrote the story when I was at home, the autumn after I had learnt to speak. We had stayed up at Fern Quarry later than usual. While we were there, Miss Sullivan had described to me the beauties of the late foliage, and it seems that her descriptions revived the memory of a story, which must have been read to me, and which I must have unconsciously retained. I thought then that I was "making up a story," as children say, and I eagerly sat down to write it before the ideas should slip from me. My thoughts flowed easily; I felt a sense of joy in the composition. Words and images came tripping to my finger ends, and as I thought out sentence after sentence, I wrote them on my Braille slate. Now, if words and images come to me without effort, it is a pretty sure sign that they are not the offspring of my own mind, but stray waifs that I regretfully dismiss. At that time I eagerly absorbed everything I read without a thought of authorship, and even now I cannot be quite sure of the boundary line between my ideas and those I find in books. I suppose that is because so many of my impressions come to me through the medium of others' eyes and ears.

When the story was finished, I read it to my teacher, and I recall now vividly the pleasure I felt in the more beautiful passages, and my annoyance at being interrupted to have the pronunciation of a word corrected. At dinner it was read to the assembled family, who were surprised that I could write so well. Someone asked me if I had read it in a book.

When the story was finished, I read it to my teacher, and I recall now vividly the pleasure I felt in the more beautiful passages, and my annoyance at being interrupted to have the pronunciation of a word corrected. At dinner it was read to the assembled family, who were surprised that I could write so well. Someone asked me if I had read it in a book.

This question surprised me very much; for I had not the faintest recollection of having had it read to me. I spoke up and said, "Oh, no, it is my story, and I have written it for Mr. Anagnos."

Accordingly I copied the story and sent it to him for his birthday. It was suggested that I should change the title from "Autumn Leaves" to "The Frost King," which I did. I carried the little story to the post-office myself, feeling as if I were walking on air. I little dreamed how cruelly I would have to pay for that birthday gift.

Mr. Anagnos was delighted with "The Frost King," and

published it in one of the Perkins Institution reports. This was the pinnacle of my happiness, from which I was in a little while dashed to earth. I had been in Boston only a short time when it was discovered that a story similar to "The Frost King," called "The Frost Fairies" by Miss Margaret T. Canby, had appeared before I was born in a book called "Birdie and His Friends." The two stories were so much alike in thought and language that it was evident Miss Canby's story had been read to me, and that mine was—a plagiarism. It was difficult to make me understand this; but when I did understand I was astonished and grieved. No child ever drank deeper of the cup of bitterness than I did. I had disgraced myself; I had brought suspicion upon those I loved best. And yet how could it possibly have happened? I racked my brain until I was weary to recall anything about the frost that I had read before I wrote "The Frost King"; but I could remember nothing, except the common reference to Jack Frost, and a poem for children, "The Freaks of the Frost," and I knew I had not used that in my composition.

This was the pinnacle of my happiness, from which I was in a little while dashed to earth. I had been in Boston only a short time when it was discovered that a story similar to "The Frost King," called "The Frost Fairies" by Miss Margaret T. Canby, had appeared before I was born in a book called "Birdie and His Friends."

At first Mr. Anagnos, though deeply troubled, seemed to believe me. He was unusually tender and kind to me, and for a brief space the shadow lifted. To please him I tried not to be unhappy, and to make myself as pretty as possible for the celebration of Washington's birthday, which took place very soon after I received the sad news.

I was to be Ceres in a kind of masque given by the blind girls. How well I remember the graceful draperies that enfolded me, the bright autumn leaves that wreathed my head, and the fruit and grain at my feet and in my hands, and beneath all the piety of the masque the oppressive sense of coming ill that made my heart heavy.

The night before the celebration, one of the teachers of the Institution had asked me a question connected with "The Frost King," and I was telling her that Miss Sullivan had talked to me about Jack Frost and his wonderful works. Something I said made her think she detected in my words a confession that I did remember Miss Canby's story of "The Frost Fairies," and she laid her conclusions before Mr. Anagnos, although I had told her most emphatically that she was mistaken.

The night before the celebration, one of the teachers of the Institution had asked me a question connected with "The Frost King," and I was telling her that Miss Sullivan had talked to me about Jack Frost and his wonderful works.

Mr. Anagnos, who loved me tenderly, thinking that he had been deceived, turned a deaf ear to the pleadings of love and innocence. He believed, or at least suspected, that Miss Sullivan and I had deliberately stolen the bright thoughts of another and imposed them on him to win his admiration. I was brought before a court of investigation composed of the teachers and officers of the Institution, and Miss Sullivan was asked to leave me. Then I was questioned and cross-questioned with what seemed to me a determination on the part of my judges to force me to acknowledge that I remembered having had "The Frost Fairies" read to me. I felt in every question the doubt and suspicion that was in their minds, and I felt, too, that a loved friend was looking at me reproachfully, although I could not have put all this into words. The blood pressed about my thumping heart, and I could scarcely speak, except in monosyllables. Even the consciousness that it was only a dreadful mistake did not lessen my suffering, and when at last I was allowed to leave the room, I was dazed and did not notice my teacher's caresses, or the tender words of my friends, who said that I was a brave little girl and they were proud of me.

As I lay in my bed that night, I wept as I hope few children have wept. I felt so cold, I imagined I would die before morning, and the thought comforted me. I think if this sorrow had come to me when I was older, it would have broken my spirit beyond repairing. But the angel of forgetfulness has gathered up and carried away much of the misery and all the bitterness of those sad days.

As I lay in my bed that night, I wept as I hope few children have wept. I felt so cold, I imagined I would die before morning, and the thought comforted me. I think if this sorrow had come to me when I was older, it would have broken my spirit beyond repairing. But the angel of forgetfulness has gathered up and carried away much of the misery and all the bitterness of those sad days.

Miss Sullivan had never heard of "The Frost Fairies" or of the book in which it was published. With the assistance of Dr. Alexander Graham Bell, she investigated the matter carefully, and at last it came out that Mrs. Sophia C. Hopkins had a copy of Miss Canby's "Birdie and His Friends" in 1888, the year that we spent the summer with her at Brewster. Mrs. Hopkins was unable to find her copy; but she has told me that at that time, while Miss Sullivan was away on a vacation, she had tried to amuse me by reading from various books, and although she could not remember reading "The Frost Fairies" any more than I, yet she felt sure that "Birdie and His Friends" was one of them. She explained the disappearance of the book by the fact that she had a short time before sold her house and disposed of many juvenile books, such as old schoolbooks and fairy tales, and that "Birdie and His Friends" was probably among them.

Hopkins was unable to find her copy; but she has told me that at that time, while Miss Sullivan was away on a vacation, she had tried to amuse me by reading from various books, and although she could not remember reading "The Frost Fairies" any more than I, yet she felt sure that "Birdie and His Friends" was one of them.

The stories had little or no meaning for me then; but the mere spelling of the strange words was sufficient to amuse a little child who could do almost nothing to amuse herself; and although I do not recall a single circumstance connected with the reading of the stories, yet I cannot help thinking that I made a great effort to remember the words, with the intention of having my teacher explain them when she returned. One thing is certain; the language was ineffaceably stamped upon my brain, though for a long time no one knew it, least of all myself.

When Miss Sullivan came back, I did not speak to her about "The Frost Fairies," probably because she began at once to read "Little Lord Fauntleroy," which filled my mind to the exclusion of everything else. But the fact remains that Miss Canby's story was read to me once, and that long after I had forgotten it, it came back to me so naturally that I never suspected that it was the child of another mind. In my trouble I received many messages of love and sympathy. All the friends I loved best, except one, have remained my own to the present time.

Miss Canby herself wrote kindly, "Some day you will write a great story out of your own head, that will be a comfort and help to many." But this kind prophecy has never been fulfilled. I have never played with words again for the mere pleasure of the game. Indeed, I have ever since been tortured by the fear that what I write is not my own. For a long time, when I wrote a letter, even to my mother, I was seized with a sudden feeling of terror, and I would spell the sentences over and over, to make sure that I had not read them in a book. Had it not been for the persistent encouragement of Miss Sullivan, I think I would have given up trying to write altogether.

Miss Canby herself wrote kindly, "Some day you will write a great story out of your own head, that will be a comfort and help to many." But this kind prophecy has never been fulfilled. I have never played with words again for the mere pleasure of the game. Indeed, I have ever since been tortured by the fear that what I write is not my own.

I have read "The Frost Fairies" since, also the letters I wrote in which I used other ideas of Miss Canby's. I find in one of them, a letter to Mr. Anagnos, dated September 29, 1891, words and sentiments exactly like those of the book. At the time I was writing "The Frost King," and this letter, like many others, contains phrases, which show that my mind was saturated with the story. I represent my teacher as saying to me of the golden autumn leaves, "Yes, they are beautiful enough to comfort us for the flight of summer"—an idea direct from Miss Canby's story.

This habit of assimilating what pleased me and giving it out again as my own appears in much of my early correspondence and my first attempts at writing. In a composition which I wrote about the old cities of Greece and Italy, I borrowed my glowing descriptions, with variations, from sources I have forgotten. I knew Mr. Anagnos's great love of antiquity and his enthusiastic appreciation of all beautiful sentiments about Italy and Greece. I therefore gathered from all the books I read every bit of poetry or of history that I thought would give him pleasure. Mr. Anagnos, in speaking of my composition on the cities, has said, "These ideas are poetic in their essence." But I do not understand how he ever thought a blind and deaf child of eleven could have invented them. Yet I cannot think that because I did not originate the ideas, my little composition is therefore quite devoid of interest. It shows me

This habit of assimilating what pleased me and giving it out again as my own appears in much of my early correspondence and my first attempts at writing. In a composition which I wrote about the old cities of Greece and Italy, I borrowed my glowing descriptions, with variations, from sources I have forgotten.

that I could express my appreciation of beautiful and poetic ideas in clear and animated language.

Those early compositions were mental gymnastics. I was learning, as all young and inexperienced persons learn, by assimilation and imitation, to put ideas into words. Consciously or unconsciously, I retained in my memory everything I found in books that pleased me, and adapted it. The young writer, as Stevenson has said, instinctively tries to copy whatever seems most admirable, and he shifts his admiration with astonishing versatility. It is only after years of this sort of practice that even great men have learnt to marshal the legion of words, which come thronging through every byway of the mind.

Those early compositions were mental gymnastics. I was learning, as all young and inexperienced persons learn, by assimilation and imitation, to put ideas into words. Consciously or unconsciously, I retained in my memory everything I found in books that pleased me, and adapted it.

I am afraid I have not yet completed this process. It is certain that I cannot always distinguish my own thoughts from those I read, because what I read becomes the very substance and texture of my mind. Consequently, in nearly all that I write, I produce something, which very much resembles the crazy patchwork I used to make when I first learnt to sew. This patchwork was made of all sorts of odds and ends—pretty bits of silk and velvet; but the coarse pieces that were not pleasant to touch always predominated. Likewise my compositions are made up of crude notions of my own, inlaid with the brighter thoughts and riper opinions of the authors I have read. It seems to me that the great difficulty of writing is to make the language of the educated mind express our confused ideas, half feelings, half thoughts, when we are little more than bundles of instinctive tendencies. Trying to write is very much like trying to put a Chinese puzzle together. We have a pattern in mind, which we wish to work out in words; but the words will not fit the spaces, or, if they do, they will not match the design. But we keep on trying because we know that others have succeeded, and we are not willing to acknowledge defeat.

"There is no way to become original, except to be born so," says Stevenson, and although I may not be original, I hope sometime to outgrow my artificial, periwig compositions. Then, perhaps, my own thoughts and experiences will come to the surface.

"There is no way to become original, except to be born so," says Stevenson, and although I may not be original, I hope sometime to outgrow my artificial, periwig compositions. Then, perhaps, my own thoughts and experiences will come to the surface. Meanwhile I trust and hope and persevere, and try not to let the bitter memory of "The Frost King" trammel my efforts.

So this sad experience may have done me good and set me thinking on some of the problems of composition. My only regret is that it resulted in the loss of one of my dearest friends, Mr. Anagnos.

After the publication of "The Story of My Life" in the *Ladies' Home Journal,* Mr. Anagnos had made a statement in a letter to Mr. Macy, that at the time of the "Frost King" matter, he had believed I was innocent. He says the court of investigation before which I was brought consisted of eight people: four blind, four seeing persons. Four of them, he says, thought that I knew that Miss Canby's story had been read to me, and the others did not hold this view. Mr. Anagnos states that he cast his vote with those who were favourable to me.

But, however the case may have been, with whichever side he may have cast his vote, when I went into the room where Mr. Anagnos had so often held me on his knee and, forgetting his many cares, had shared in my frolics, and found there persons who seemed to doubt me, I felt that there was something hostile and menacing in the very atmosphere, and subsequent events have borne out this impression. For two years he seems to have held the belief that Miss Sullivan and I were innocent. Then he evidently retracted his favourable judgement, why I do not know. Nor did I know the details of the investigation. I never knew even the names of the members of the "court" who did not speak to me. I was too excited to notice anything, too frightened to ask questions. Indeed, I could scarcely think what I was saying, or what was being said to me.

But, however the case may have been, with whichever side he may have cast his vote, when I went into the room where Mr. Anagnos had so often held me on his knee and, forgetting his many cares, had shared in my frolics, and found there persons who seemed to doubt me, I felt that there was something hostile and menacing in the very atmosphere, and subsequent events have borne out this impression.

I have given this account of the "Frost King" affair

because it was important in my life and education; and, in order that there might be no misunderstanding, I have set forth all the facts as they appear to me, without a thought of defending myself or of laying blame on anyone.

□

15

I spent the summer and winter following the "Frost King" incident with my family in Alabama. I recall with delight that home going. Everything had budded and blossomed. I was happy. "The Frost King" was forgotten.

When the ground was strewn with the crimson and golden leaves of autumn, and the musk-scented grapes that covered the arbour at the end of the garden were turning golden brown in the sunshine, I began to write a sketch of my life—a year after I had written "The Frost King."

I was still excessively scrupulous about everything I wrote. The thought that what I wrote might not be absolutely my own, tormented me. No one knew of these fears except my teacher. A strange sensitiveness prevented me from referring to the "Frost King"; and often when an idea flashed out in the course of conversation I would spell softly to her, "I am not sure it is mine." At other times, in the midst of a paragraph I was writing, I said to myself, "Suppose it should be found that all this was written by someone long ago!" An impish fear clutched my hand, so that I could not write any more that day. And even now I sometimes feel the same uneasiness and disquietude.

Miss Sullivan consoled and helped me in every way she could think of; but the terrible experience I had passed through left a lasting impression on my mind, the significance of which I am only just beginning to understand. It was with the hope of restoring my self-confidence that she persuaded me to write a brief account of my life for the *Youth's Companion*. I was then twelve years old. As I look back on my struggle to write that little story, it seems to me that I must have had a prophetic vision of the good that would come of the undertaking, or I would surely have failed.

I wrote timidly, fearfully, but resolutely, urged on by my teacher, who knew that if I persevered, I would find my mental foothold again and get a grip on my faculties. Up to the time of the "Frost King" episode, I had lived the unconscious life of a little child. Now my thoughts were turned inwards, and I beheld things invisible. Gradually I emerged from the penumbra of that experience with a mind made clearer by trial and with a truer knowledge of life.

I wrote timidly, fearfully, but resolutely, urged on by my teacher, who knew that if I persevered, I would find my mental foothold again and get a grip on my faculties. Up to the time of the "Frost King" episode, I had lived the unconscious life of a little child. Now my thoughts were turned inwards, and I beheld things invisible.

The chief events of the year 1893 were my trip to Washington during the inauguration of President Cleveland, and visits to Niagara and the World's Fair. Under such circumstances my studies were constantly interrupted and often put aside for many weeks and so it is impossible for me to give a connected account of them.

We went to Niagara in March 1893. It is difficult to describe my emotions when I stood on the point which overhangs the American Falls, and felt the air vibrate and the earth tremble.

It seems strange to many people that I should be impressed by the wonders and beauties of Niagara. They are always asking: "What does this beauty or that music mean to you? You cannot see the waves rolling up the beach or hear their roar. What do they mean to you?" In the most evident sense they mean everything. I cannot fathom or define their meaning any more than I can fathom or define love or religion or goodness.

It seems strange to many people that I should be impressed by the wonders and beauties of Niagara. They are always asking: "What does this beauty or that music mean to you? You cannot see the waves rolling up the beach or hear their roar. What do they mean to you?" In the most evident sense they mean everything.

During the summer of 1893, Miss Sullivan and I visited the World's Fair with Dr. Alexander Graham Bell. I recall with unmixed delight those days when a thousand childish fancies became beautiful realities. Every day in imagination I made a trip round the world, and I saw many wonders from the uttermost parts of the earth—marvels of invention, treasuries of industry and skill, and all the activities of human life actually passed under my finger tips.

I liked to visit the Midway Plaisance. It seemed like the "Arabian Nights." It was crammedfull of novelty and interest. Here was the India of my books in the curious bazaar with its Shivas and elephant-gods; there was the land of the Pyramids concentrated in a model Cairo with its mosques and its long processions of camels; yonder were the lagoons of Venice, where we sailed every evening when the city and the fountains were illuminated.

I also went on board a Viking ship, which lay a short distance from the little craft. I had been on a man-of-war before, in Boston, and it interested me to see, on this Viking ship, how the seaman was once all in all—how he sailed and took storm and calm alike with undaunted heart, and gave chase to whosoever reechoed his cry, "We are of the sea!" and fought with brains and sinews, self-reliant, self-sufficient, instead of being thrust into the background by unintelligent machinery, as Jack is today. So it always is—"man only is interesting to man."

At a little distance from this ship there was a model of the *Santa Maria*, which I also examined. The captain showed me Columbus's cabin and the desk with an hourglass on it. This small instrument impressed me most because it made me think how weary the heroic navigator must have felt as he saw the sand dropping grain by grain while desperate men were plotting against his life.

At a little distance from this ship there was a model of the Santa Maria, which I also examined. The captain showed me Columbus's cabin and the desk with an hourglass on it. This small instrument impressed me most because it made me think how weary the heroic navigator must have felt as he saw the sand dropping grain by grain while desperate men were plotting against his life.

Mr. Higinbotham, President of the World's Fair, kindly gave me permission to touch the exhibits, and with eagerness as insatiable as that with which Pizarro seized the treasures of

Peru, I took in the glories of the Fair with my fingers. It was a sort of tangible kaleidoscope, this white city of the West. Everything fascinated me, especially the French bronzes. They were so lifelike that I thought they were angel visions, which the artist had caught and bound in earthly forms.

At the Cape of Good Hope exhibit, I learnt much about the processes of mining diamonds. Whenever it was possible, I touched the machinery while it was in motion, so as to get a clearer idea of how the stones were weighed, cut, and polished. I searched in the washings for a diamond and found it myself—the only true diamond, they said, that was ever found in the United States.

At the Cape of Good Hope exhibit, I learnt much about the processes of mining diamonds. Whenever it was possible, I touched the machinery while it was in motion, so as to get a clearer idea of how the stones were weighed, cut, and polished.

Dr. Bell went everywhere with us and in his own delightful way described to me the objects of greatest interest. In the electrical building we examined the telephones, autophones, phonographs, and other inventions, and he made me understand how it is possible to send a message on wires that mock space and outrun time, and, like Prometheus, draw fire from the sky.

We also visited the anthropological department, and I was much interested in the relics of ancient Mexico, in the rude stone implements that are so often the only record of an age—the simple monuments of Nature's unlettered children (so I thought as I fingered them) that seem bound to last while the memorials of kings and sages crumble away in dust—and in the Egyptian mummies, which I shrank from touching. From these relics I learnt more about the progress of man than I have heard or read since.

All these experiences added a great many new terms to my vocabulary, and in the three weeks I spent at the Fair I took a long leap from the little child's interest in fairy tales and toys to the appreciation of the real and the earnest in the work-a-day world.

□

16

By October 1893, I had studied various subjects by myself in a more or less desultory manner. I read the histories of Greece, Rome and the United States. I had a French grammar in raised print, and as I already knew some French, I often amused myself by composing in my head short exercises, using the new words as I came across them, and ignoring rules and other technicalities as much as possible. I even tried, without aid, to master the French pronunciation, as I found all the letters and sounds described in the book. Of course this was tasking slender powers for great ends; but it gave me something to do on a rainy day, and I acquired a sufficient knowledge of French to read with pleasure La Fontaine's "Fables," "Le Medecin Malgre Lui" and passages from "Athalie."

I also gave considerable time to the improvement of my speech. I read aloud to Miss Sullivan and recited passages from my favourite poets, which I had committed to memory. She corrected my pronunciation and helped me to phrase and inflect. It was not, however, until October 1893, after I had recovered from the fatigue and excitement of my visit to the World's Fair, that I began to have lessons in special subjects at fixed hours.

Miss Sullivan and I were at that time in Hulton, Pennsylvania, visiting the family of Mr. William Wade. Mr. Irons, a neighbour of theirs, was a good Latin scholar. It was arranged that I should study under him. I remember him as a man of rare, sweet nature and of wide experience. He taught me Latin grammar principally; but he often helped me in arithmetic, which I found as troublesome as it was uninteresting. Mr. Irons also read with me Tennyson's "In Memoriam." I had read many books before, but never from a critical point of view. I learnt for the first time to know an author, to recognise his style as I recognise the clasp of a friend's hand.

At first I was rather unwilling to study Latin grammar. It seemed absurd to waste time analysing, every word I came across—noun, genitive, singular, feminine—when its meaning was quite plain. I thought I might just as well describe my pet in order to know it—order, vertebrate; division, quadruped; class, mammalia; genus, felinus; species, cat; individual, Tabby. But as I got deeper into the subject, I became more interested, and the beauty of the language delighted me. I often amused myself by reading Latin passages or picking up words I understood and trying to make sense. I have never ceased to enjoy this pastime.

At first I was rather unwilling to study Latin grammar. It seemed absurd to waste time analysing, every word I came across—noun, genitive, singular, feminine—when its meaning was quite plain. I thought I might just as well describe my pet in order to know it—order, vertebrate; division, quadruped; class, mammalia; genus, felinus; species, cat; individual, Tabby.

There is nothing more beautiful, I think, than the evanescent fleeting images and sentiments presented by a language one is just becoming familiar with—ideas that flit across the mental sky, shaped and tinted by capricious fancy. Miss Sullivan sat beside me at my lessons, spelling into my hand whatever Mr. Irons said, and looking up for new words for me. I was just beginning to read Caesar's "Gallic War" when I went to my home in Alabama.

□

17

In the summer of 1894, I attended the meeting at Chautauqua of the American Association to Promote the Teaching of Speech to the Deaf. There it was arranged that I should go to the Wright-Humason School for the Deaf in New York City. I went there in October 1894, accompanied by Miss Sullivan. This school was chosen especially for the purpose of obtaining the highest advantages in vocal culture and training in lip-reading. In addition to my work in these subjects, I studied arithmetic, physical geography, French and German, during the two years I was in the school.

Miss Reamy, my German teacher, could use the manual alphabet, and after I had acquired a small vocabulary, we talked together in German whenever we had a chance, and in a few months I could understand almost everything she said. Before the end of the first year I read "Wilhelm Tell" with the greatest delight. Indeed, I think I made more progress in German than in any of my other studies. I found French much more difficult. I studied it with Madame Olivier, a French lady who did not know the manual alphabet, and who was obliged to give her instruction orally. I could not read her lips easily; so my progress was much slower than in German. I managed, however, to read "Le Medecin Malgre Lui" again. It was very amusing but I did not like it nearly so well as "Wilhelm Tell."

My progress in lip-reading and speech was not what my teachers and I had hoped and expected it would be. It was my ambition to speak like other people, and my teachers believed that this could be accomplished; but, although we worked hard and faithfully, yet we did not quite reach our goal. I suppose we aimed too high, and disappointment was therefore inevitable. I still regarded arithmetic as a system of pitfalls. I hung about the dangerous frontier of "guess," avoiding with infinite trouble to others and myself the broad valley of reason. When I was not guessing, I was jumping at conclusions, and this fault, in addition to my dullness, aggravated my difficulties more than was right or necessary.

I still regarded arithmetic as a system of pitfalls. I hung about the dangerous frontier of "guess," avoiding with infinite trouble to others and myself the broad valley of reason. When I was not guessing, I was jumping at conclusions, and this fault, in addition to my dullness, aggravated my difficulties more than was right or necessary.

But although these disappointments caused me great depression at times, I pursued my other studies with unflagging interest, especially physical geography. It was a joy to learn the secrets of Nature: how—in the picturesque language of the Old Testament—the winds are made to blow from the four corners of the heavens, how the vapours ascend from the ends of the earth, how rivers are cut out among the rocks, and mountains overturned by the roots, and in what ways man may overcome many forces mightier than himself. The two years in New York were happy ones, and I look back to them with genuine pleasure.

I remember especially the walks we all took together

every day in Central Park, the only part of the city that was congenial to me. I never lost a jot of my delight in this great park. I loved to have it described every time I entered it; for it was beautiful in all its aspects, and these aspects were so many that it was beautiful in a different way each day of the nine months I spent in New York.

In the spring we made excursions to various places of interest. We sailed on the Hudson River and wandered about on its green banks, of which Bryant loved to sing. I liked the simple, wild grandeur of the palisades. Among the places I visited were West Point, Tarrytown, the home of Washington Irving, where I walked through 'Sleepy Hollow.'

In the spring we made excursions to various places of interest. We sailed on the Hudson River and wandered about on its green banks, of which Bryant loved to sing. I liked the simple, wild grandeur of the palisades. Among the places I visited were West Point, Tarrytown, the home of Washington Irving, where I walked through 'Sleepy Hollow.'

The teachers at the Wright-Humason School were always planning how they might give the pupils every advantage that those who hear enjoy—how they might make much of few tendencies and passive memories in the cases of the little ones—lead them out of the cramping circumstances in which their lives were set.

Before I left New York, these bright days were darkened by the greatest sorrow that I have ever borne, except the death of my father. Mr. John P. Spaulding, of Boston, died in February 1896. Only those who knew and loved him best can understand what his friendship had meant to me. He, who made everyone happy in a beautiful, unobtrusive way, was most kind and tender to Miss Sullivan and me. So long as we felt his loving presence and knew that he took a watchful interest in our work, fraught with so many difficulties, we could not be discouraged. His going away left a vacancy in our lives that has never been filled.

□

18

In October, 1896, I entered the Cambridge School for Young Ladies, to be prepared for Radcliffe.

When I was a little girl, I had visited Wellesley and surprised my friends by the announcement, "Some day I shall go to college—but I shall go to Harvard!" When asked why I would not go to Wellesley, I replied that there were only girls there. The thought of going to college took root in my heart and became an earnest desire, which impelled me to enter into competition for a degree with seeing and hearing girls, in the face of the strong opposition of many true and wise friends. When I left New York the idea had become a fixed purpose; and it was decided that I should go to Cambridge. This was the nearest approach I could get to Harvard and to the fulfilment of my childish declaration.

At the Cambridge School, the plan was to have Miss Sullivan attend the classes with me and interpret to me the instruction given.

Of course my instructors had no experience in teaching but normal pupils, and my only means of conversing with them was reading their lips. My studies for the first year were English history, English literature, German, Latin, Arithmetic, Latin composition and occasional themes. Until then I had never taken a course of study with the idea of preparing for college; but I had been well drilled in English by Miss Sullivan, and it soon became evident to my teachers that I needed no special instruction in this subject beyond a critical study of the books prescribed by the college. I had, moreover, a good start in French, and received six months' instruction in Latin; but German was the subject with which I was most familiar.

However, in spite of these advantages, there were serious drawbacks to my progress. Miss Sullivan could not spell out in my hand all that the books required, and it was very difficult to have textbooks embossed in time to be of use to me, although my friends in London and Philadelphia were willing to hasten the work. For a while, indeed, I had to copy my Latin in Braille, so that I could recite with the other girls. My instructors soon became sufficiently familiar with my imperfect speech, my eagerness to answer my questions readily and correct mistakes. I could not make notes in class or write exercises; but I wrote all my compositions and translations at home on my typewriter.

However, in spite of these advantages, there were serious drawbacks to my progress. Miss Sullivan could not spell out in my hand all that the books required, and it was very difficult to have textbooks embossed in time to be of use to me, although my friends in London and Philadelphia were willing to hasten the work.

Each day Miss Sullivan went to the classes with me and spelled into my hand with infinite patience all that the teachers said. In study hours she had to look up new words for me, and read and reread notes and books I did not have in raised print. The tedium of that work is hard to conceive. Frau Grote, my German teacher, and Mr. Gilman, the principal, were the only teachers in the school who learnt the finger alphabet to give me instruction. No one realized more fully than dear Frau Grote how slow and inadequate her spelling was. Nevertheless, in the goodness of her heart she laboriously spelled out her instructions to me in special lessons twice a week, to give Miss Sullivan a little rest. But, though everybody was kind and ready to help us, there was only one hand that could turn drudgery into pleasure.

That year I finished arithmetic, reviewed my Latin grammar, and read three chapters of Caesar's "Gallic War." In German I read, partly with my fingers and partly with Miss Sullivan's assistance, Schiller's "Lied von der Glocke" and "Taucher," Heine's "Harzreise," Freytag's "Aus dem Staat Friedrichs des Grossen," Riehl's "Fluch Der Schonheit," Lessing's "Minna von Barnhelm," and Goethe's "Aus meinem Leben."

That year I finished arithmetic, reviewed my Latin grammar, and read three chapters of Caesar's "Gallic War." In German I read, partly with my fingers and partly with Miss Sullivan's assistance, Schiller's "Lied von der Glocke" and "Taucher," Heine's "Harzreise," Freytag's "Aus dem Staat Friedrichs des Grossen," Riehl's "Fluch Der Schonheit," Lessing's "Minna von Barnhelm," and Goethe's "Aus meinem Leben." I took the greatest delight in these German books, especially Schiller's wonderful lyrics, the history of Frederick the Great's magnificent achievements and the account of Goethe's life. I was sorry to finish "Die Harzreise," so full of happy witticisms and charming descriptions of vine-clad hills, streams that sing and ripple in the sunshine, and wild regions, sacred to tradition and legend, the grey sisters of a long-vanished, imaginative age—descriptions such as can be given only by those to whom Nature is "a feeling, a love and an appetite."

Mr. Gilman instructed me for a part of the year in English literature. We read together, "As You Like It," Burke's "Speech on Conciliation with America," and Macaulay's "Life of Samuel Johnson." Mr. Gilman's broad views of history and literature and his clever explanations made my work easier and pleasanter than it could have been had I only read notes mechanically with the necessarily brief explanations given in the classes.

Burke's speech was more instructive than any other book on a political subject that I had ever read. My mind stirred with the stirring times, and the characters round which the life of two contending nations centered seemed to move right before me.

Burke's speech was more instructive than any other book on a political subject that I had ever read. My mind stirred with the stirring times, and the characters round which the life of two contending nations centered seemed to move right before me. I wondered more and more, while Burke's masterly speech rolled on in mighty surges of eloquence, how it was that King George and his ministers could have turned a deaf ear to his warning prophecy of our victory and their humiliation. Then I entered into the melancholy details of the relation in which the great statesman stood to his party and to the representatives of the people. I thought how strange it was that such precious seeds of truth and wisdom should have fallen among the tares of ignorance and corruption.

In a different way Macaulay's "Life of Samuel Johnson" was interesting. My heart went out to the lonely man who ate the bread of affliction in Grub Street, and yet, in the midst of toil and cruel suffering of body and soul, always had a kind word, and lent a helping hand to the poor and despised. I rejoiced over all his successes, I shut my eyes to his faults, and wondered, not that he had them, but that they had not crushed or dwarfed his soul. But in spite of Macaulay's brilliancy and his admirable faculty of making the commonplace seem fresh and picturesque, his positivist approach wearied me at times, and his frequent sacrifices of truth to effect kept me in a questioning attitude very unlike the attitude of reverence in which I had listened to the Demosthenes of Great Britain.

In a different way Macaulay's "Life of Samuel Johnson" was interesting. My heart went out to the lonely man who ate the bread of affliction in Grub Street, and yet, in the midst of toil and cruel suffering of body and soul, always had a kind word, and lent a helping hand to the poor and despised.

At the Cambridge school, for the first time in my life, I enjoyed the companionship of seeing and hearing girls of my own age. I lived with several others in one of the pleasant houses connected with the school, the house where Mr. Howells used to live, and we all had the advantage of home life. I joined them in many of their games, even blind man's buff and frolics in the snow; I took long walks with them; we discussed our studies and read aloud the things that interested us. Some of the girls learnt to speak to me, so that Miss Sullivan did not have to repeat their conversation.

At Christmas, my mother and little sister spent the

holidays with me, and Mr. Gilman kindly offered to let Mildred study in his school. So Mildred stayed with me in Cambridge, and for six happy months we were hardly ever apart. It makes me most happy to remember the hours we spent helping each other in study and sharing our recreation together.

I took my preliminary examinations for Radcliffe from the 29th of June to the 3rd of July in 1897. The subjects I offered were Elementary and Advanced German, French, Latin, English, and Greek and Roman history, making nine hours in all. I passed in everything, and received "honours" in German and English.

I took my preliminary examinations for Radcliffe from the 29th of June to the 3rd of July in 1897. The subjects I offered were Elementary and Advanced German, French, Latin, English, and Greek and Roman history, making nine hours in all. I passed in everything, and received "honours" in German and English.

Perhaps an explanation of the method that was in use when I took my examinations will not be amiss here. The student was required to pass in sixteen hours—twelve hours being called elementary and four advanced. He had to pass five hours at a time to have them counted. The examination papers were given out at nine o'clock at Harvard and brought to Radcliffe by a special messenger. Each candidate was known, not by his name, but by a number. I was No. 233, but, as I had to use a typewriter, my identity could not be concealed.

It was thought advisable for me to have my examinations in a room by myself, because the noise of the typewriter might disturb the other girls. Mr. Gilman read all the papers to me by means of the manual alphabet. A man was placed on guard at the door to prevent interruption.

The first day I had German. Mr. Gilman sat beside me and read the paper through first, then sentence by sentence, while I repeated the words aloud, to make sure that I understood him perfectly. The papers were difficult, and I felt very anxious as I wrote out my answers on the typewriter. Mr. Gilman spelled to me what I had written, and I made such changes as I thought necessary, and he inserted them. I wish to say here that I have not had this advantage since in any of my examinations. At Radcliffe no one reads the papers to me after they are written, and I have no opportunity to correct errors unless I finish before the time is up. In that case I correct only such mistakes as I can recall in the few minutes allowed, and make notes of these corrections at the end of my paper. If I passed with higher credit in the preliminaries than in the finals, there are two reasons. In the finals, no one read my work over to me, and in the preliminaries I offered subjects with some of which I was in a measure familiar before my work in the Cambridge School; for at the beginning of the year I had passed examinations in English, History, French and German, which Mr. Gilman gave me from previous Harvard Papers.

The first day I had German. Mr. Gilman sat beside me and read the paper through first, then sentence by sentence, while I repeated the words aloud, to make sure that I understood him perfectly. The papers were difficult, and I felt very anxious as I wrote out my answers on the typewriter.

Mr. Gilman sent my written work to the examiners with

a certificate that I, candidate No. 233, had written the Papers.

All the other preliminary examinations were conducted in the same manner. None of them was as difficult as the first. I remember that the day the Latin paper was brought to us; Professor Schilling came in and informed me that I had passed satisfactorily in German. This encouraged me greatly, and I sped on to the end of the ordeal with a light heart and a steady hand.

□

19

When I began my second year at the Gilman school, I was full of hope and determination to succeed. But during the first few weeks I was confronted with unforeseen difficulties. Mr. Gilman had agreed that, that year I should study mathematics principally. I had physics, algebra, geometry, astronomy, Greek and Latin. Unfortunately, many of the books I needed had not been embossed in time for me to begin with the classes, and I lacked important apparatus for some of my studies. The classes I was in were very large, and it was impossible for the teachers to give me special instruction. Miss Sullivan was obliged to read all the books to me, and interpret for the instructors, and for the first time in eleven years it seemed as if her dear hand would not be equal to the task.

It was necessary for me to write algebra and geometry in class and solve problems in physics, and this I could not do until we bought a Braillewriter, by means of which I could put down the steps and processes of my work. I could not follow with my eyes the geometrical figures drawn on the blackboard, and my only means of getting a clear idea of them was to make them on a cushion with straight and curved wires, which had bent and pointed ends. I had to carry in my mind, as Mr. Keith says in his report, the lettering of the figures, the hypothesis and conclusion, the construction and the process of the proof. In a word, every study had its obstacles. Sometimes I lost all courage and betrayed my feelings in a way I am ashamed to remember, especially as the signs of my trouble were afterwards used against Miss Sullivan, the only person of all the kind friends I had there, who could make the crooked straight and the rough places smooth.

Little by little, however, my difficulties began to disappear. The embossed books and other apparatus arrived, and I threw myself into the work with renewed confidence. Algebra and geometry were the only studies that continued to defy my efforts to comprehend them. As I have said before, I had no aptitude for mathematics; the different points were not explained to me as fully as I wished.

Little by little, however, my difficulties began to disappear. The embossed books and other apparatus arrived, and I threw myself into the work with renewed confidence. Algebra and geometry were the only studies that continued to defy my efforts to comprehend them. As I have said before, I had no aptitude for mathematics; the different points were not explained to me as fully as I wished. The geometrical diagrams were particularly vexing because I could not see the relation of the different parts to one another, even on the cushion. It was not until Mr. Keith taught me that I had a clear idea of mathematics.

I was beginning to overcome these difficulties when an event occurred which changed everything.

Just before the books came, Mr. Gilman had begun to remonstrate with Miss Sullivan on the ground that I was working too hard, and in spite of my earnest protestations;

he reduced the number of my recitations. At the beginning we had agreed that I should, if necessary, take five years to prepare for college, but at the end of the first year the success of my examinations showed Miss Sullivan, Miss Harbaugh (Mr. Gilman's head teacher), and one other, that I could without too much effort complete my preparation in two years more. Mr. Gilman at first agreed to this; but when my tasks had become somewhat perplexing, he insisted that I was overworked, and that I should remain at his school three years longer. I did not like his plan, for I wished to enter college with my class.

On the seventeenth of November I was not very well, and did not go to school. Although Miss Sullivan knew that my indisposition was not serious, yet Mr. Gilman, on hearing of it, declared that I was breaking down and made changes in my studies, which would have rendered it impossible for me to take my final examinations with my class.

On the seventeenth of November I was not very well, and did not go to school. Although Miss Sullivan knew that my indisposition was not serious, yet Mr. Gilman, on hearing of it, declared that I was breaking down and made changes in my studies, which would have rendered it impossible for me to take my final examinations with my class. In the end the difference of opinion between Mr. Gilman and Miss Sullivan resulted in my mother's withdrawing my sister Mildred and me from the Cambridge school.

After some delay it was arranged that I should continue my studies under a tutor, Mr. Merton S. Keith, of Cambridge. Miss Sullivan and I spent the rest of the winter with our friends, the Chamberlains in Wrentham, twenty-five miles from Boston.

From February to July 1898, Mr. Keith came out to Wrentham twice a week, and taught me algebra, geometry, Greek and Latin. Miss Sullivan interpreted his instruction.

In October 1898, we returned to Boston. For eight months Mr.Keith gave me lessons five times a week, in periods of about an hour. He explained each time what I did not understand in the previous lesson, assigned new work, and took home with him the Greek exercises, which I had written during the week on my typewriter, corrected them fully, and returned them to me.

In October 1898, we returned to Boston. For eight months Mr.Keith gave me lessons five times a week, in periods of about an hour. He explained each time what I did not understand in the previous lesson, assigned new work, and took home with him the Greek exercises, which I had written during the week on my typewriter, corrected them fully, and returned them to me.

In this way my preparation for college went on without interruption. I found it much easier and pleasanter to be taught by myself than to receive instruction in class. There was no hurry, no confusion. My tutor had plenty of time to explain what I did not understand, so I got on faster and did better work than I ever did in school. I still found more difficulty in mastering problems in mathematics than I did in any other of my studies. I wish algebra and geometry had been half as easy as the languages and literature. But Mr. Keith even made mathematics interesting. He succeeded in whittling problems small enough to get through my brain. He kept my mind alert and eager, and trained it to reason clearly, and to seek conclusions calmly and logically, instead of jumping wildly into space and arriving nowhere. He was always gentle and forbearing, no matter how dull I might be, and believe me, my stupidity would often have exhausted the patience of Job.

On the 29th and 30th of June, 1899, I took my final examinations for Radcliffe College. The first day I had Elementary Greek and Advanced Latin, and the second day Geometry, Algebra and Advanced Greek.

The college authorities did not allow Miss Sullivan to read the examination papers to me; so Mr. Eugene C. Vining, one of the instructors at the Perkins Institution for the Blind, was employed to copy the papers for me in American Braille. Mr. Vining was a stranger to me, and could not communicate with me, except by writing Braille. The proctor was also a stranger, and did not attempt to communicate with me in any way.

The college authorities did not allow Miss Sullivan to read the examination papers to me; so Mr. Eugene C. Vining, one of the instructors at the Perkins Institution for the Blind, was employed to copy the papers for me in American Braille. Mr. Vining was a stranger to me, and could not communicate with me, except by writing Braille.

The Braille worked well enough in the languages, but when it came to geometry and algebra, difficulties arose. I was sorely perplexed, and felt discouraged wasting much precious time, especially in algebra. It is true that I was familiar with all literary Braille in common use in this country—English, American, and New York Point; but the various signs and symbols in geometry and algebra in the three systems are very different, and I had used only the English Braille in my algebra.

Two days before the examinations, Mr. Vining sent me a Braille copy of one of the old Harvard papers in algebra. To my dismay I found that it was in the American notation. I sat down immediately and wrote to Mr. Vining, asking him to explain the signs. I received another paper and a table of signs by return mail, and I set to work to learn the notation. But on the night before the algebra examination, while I was struggling over some very complicated examples, I could not tell the combinations of bracket, brace and radical. Both Mr. Keith and I were distressed and full of forebodings for the morrow; but we went over to the college a little before the examination began, and had Mr. Vining explain more fully the American symbols.

Two days before the examinations, Mr. Vining sent me a Braille copy of one of the old Harvard papers in algebra. To my dismay I found that it was in the American notation. I sat down immediately and wrote to Mr. Vining, asking him to explain the signs.

In geometry my chief difficulty was that I had always been accustomed to read the propositions in line print, or to have them spelled into my hand; and somehow, although the propositions were right before me, I found the Braille confusing, and could not fix clearly in my mind what I was reading. But when I took up algebra I had a harder time still. The signs, which I had lately learnt, and which I thought I knew, perplexed me. Besides, I could not see what I wrote on my typewriter. I had always done my work in Braille or in my head. Mr. Keith had relied too much on my ability to solve problems mentally, and had not trained me to write examination papers. Consequently, my work was painfully slow, and I had to read the examples over and over before I could form any idea of what I was required to do. Indeed, I am not sure now that I read all the signs correctly. I found it very hard to keep my wits about me.

But I do not blame any one. The administrative board of Radcliffe did not realise how difficult they were making my examinations, nor did they understand the peculiar difficulties I had to surmount. But if they unintentionally placed obstacles in my way, I have the consolation of knowing that I overcame them all.

□

20

The struggle for admission to college ended, and I could now enter Radcliffe whenever I pleased. Before I entered college, however, it was thought best that I should study another year under Mr. Keith. It was not, therefore, until the fall of 1900 that my dream of going to college was realised.

I remember my first day at Radcliffe. It was a day full of interest for me. I had looked forward to it for years. A potent force within me, stronger than the persuasion of my friends, stronger even than the pleadings of my heart, had impelled me to try my strength by the standards of those who could see and hear. I knew that there were obstacles in the way; but I was eager to overcome them. I had taken to heart the words of the wise Roman who said, "To be banished from Rome is but to live outside of Rome." Debarred from the great highways of knowledge, I was compelled to make the journey across country by unfrequented roads—that was all; and I knew that in college there were many bypaths where I could touch hands with girls who were thinking, loving and struggling like me.

I began my studies with eagerness. Before me I saw a new world opening in beauty and light, and I felt within me the capacity to know all things. In the wonderland of Mind I should be as free as another. Its people, scenery, manners, joys, tragedies should be living, tangible interpreters of the real world. The lecture-halls seemed filled with the spirit of the great and the wise, and I thought the professors were the embodiment of wisdom. If I have since learnt differently, I am not going to tell anybody.

But I soon discovered that college was not quite the romantic lyceum I had imagined. Many of the dreams that had delighted my young inexperience became beautifully less and "faded into the light of common day." Gradually I began to find that there were disadvantages in going to college.

But I soon discovered that college was not quite the romantic lyceum I had imagined. Many of the dreams that had delighted my young inexperience became beautifully less and "faded into the light of common day." Gradually I began to find that there were disadvantages in going to college.

The one I felt and still feel most is lack of time. I used to have time to think, to reflect, my mind and I. We would sit together on an evening and listen to the inner melodies of the spirit, which one hears only in leisure moments when the words of some loved poet touch a deep, sweet chord in the soul that until then had been silent. But in college there is no time to commune with one's thoughts. One goes to college to learn, it seems, not to think. When one enters the portals of learning, one leaves the dearest pleasures—solitude, books and imagination—outside with the whispering pines. I suppose I ought to find some comfort in the thought that I am laying up treasures for future enjoyment, but I am improvident enough to prefer the present joys to hoarding riches against a rainy day.

My studies during the first year were French, German, History, English composition and English literature. In the

French course I read some of the works of Corneille, Moliere, Racine, Alfred de Musset and Sainte-Beuve, and in the German those of Goethe and Schiller. I reviewed rapidly the whole period of history from the fall of the Roman Empire to the eighteenth century, and in English literature I studied critically Milton's poems and "Areopagitica."

I am frequently asked how I overcome the peculiar conditions under which I work in college. In the classroom I am of course practically alone. The professor is as remote as if he were speaking through a telephone. The lectures are spelled into my hand as rapidly as possible, and much of the individuality of the lecturer is lost to me in the effort to keep in the race. The words rush through my hand like hounds in pursuit of a hare, which they often miss. But in this respect I do not think I am much worse off than the girls who take notes. If the mind is occupied with the mechanical process of hearing and putting words on paper at pell-mell speed, I should not think one could pay much attention to the subject under consideration or the manner in which it is presented. I cannot make notes during the lectures, because my hands are busy listening. Usually I jot down what I can remember of them when I get home. I write the exercises, daily themes, criticisms and hour-tests,

I am frequently asked how I overcome the peculiar conditions under which I work in college. In the classroom I am of course practically alone. The professor is as remote as if he were speaking through a telephone. The lectures are spelled into my hand as rapidly as possible, and much of the individuality of the lecturer is lost to me in the effort to keep in the race.

the mid-year and final examinations, on my typewriter, so that the professors have no difficulty in finding out how little I know. When I began the study of Latin prosody, I devised and explained to my professor a system of signs indicating the different metres and quantities.

I use the Hammond typewriter. I have tried many machines, and I find the Hammond is the best adapted to the peculiar needs of my work. With this machine movable type shuttles can be used, and one can have several shuttles, each with a different set of characters—Greek, French, or mathematical, according to the kind of writing one wishes to do on the typewriter. Without it, I doubt if I could go to college.

Very few of the books required in the various courses are printed for the blind, and I am obliged to have them spelled into my hand. Consequently I need more time to prepare my lessons than other girls. The manual part takes longer, and I have perplexities, which they do not have. There are days when the close attention I must give to details chafes my spirit, and the thought that I must spend hours reading a few chapters, while in the world without other girls are laughing and singing and dancing, makes me rebellious; but I soon recover my buoyancy and laugh the discontent out of my heart. For, after all, everyone who wishes to gain true knowledge must climb the Hill of Difficulty alone, and since there is no royal road to the

Very few of the books required in the various courses are printed for the blind, and I am obliged to have them spelled into my hand. Consequently I need more time to prepare my lessons than other girls. The manual part takes longer, and I have perplexities, which they do not have.

summit, I must zigzag it in my own way. I slip back many times, I fall, I stand still, I run against the edge of hidden obstacles, I lose my temper and find it again and keep it better. I trudge on, I gain a little, I feel encouraged, and I get more eager and climb higher and begin to see the widening horizon. Every struggle is a victory. One more effort and I reach the luminous cloud, the blue depths of the sky, the uplands of my desire. I am not always alone, however, in these struggles. Mr. William Wade and Mr. E. E. Allen, Principal of the Pennsylvania Institution for the Instruction of the Blind, get for me many of the books I need in raised print. Their thoughtfulness has been more of a help and encouragement to me than they can ever know.

Last year, during my second year at Radcliffe, I studied English composition, the Bible as English composition, the governments of America and Europe, the Odes of Horace, and Latin comedy. The class in composition was the most pleasant. It was very lively.

Last year, during my second year at Radcliffe, I studied English composition, the Bible as English composition, the governments of America and Europe, the Odes of Horace, and Latin comedy. The class in composition was the most pleasant. It was very lively. The lectures were always interesting, vivacious, and witty; for the instructor, Mr. Charles Townsend Copeland, more than anyone else I have until this year, brings before you literature in all its original freshness and power. For one short hour you are permitted to drink in the eternal beauty of the old masters without needless interpretation or exposition. You revel in their fine thoughts. You enjoy with all your soul the sweet thunder of the Old Testament, forgetting the existence of Jahweh and Elohim; and you go home feeling that you have had "a glimpse of that perfection in which spirit and form dwell in immortal harmony; truth and beauty bearing a new growth on the ancient stem of time."

This year is the happiest because I am studying some subjects that especially interest me like Economics, Elizabethan literature, Shakespeare under Professor George L. Kittredge, and the History of Philosophy under Professor Josiah Royce. Through philosophy one enters with sympathy of comprehension into the traditions of remote ages and other modes of thought, which some time ago seemed alien and without reason.

This year is the happiest because I am studying some subjects that especially interest me like Economics, Elizabethan literature, Shakespeare under Professor George L. Kittredge, and the History of Philosophy under Professor Josiah Royce. Through philosophy one enters with sympathy of comprehension into the traditions of remote ages and other modes of thought, which some time ago seemed alien and without reason.

But college is not the universal Athens I thought it was. There one does not meet the great and the wise face to face; one does not even feel their living touch. They are there, it is true; but they seem mummified. We must extract them from the crannied wall of learning and dissect and analyse them before we can be sure that we have a Milton or an Isaiah, and not merely a clever imitation. Many scholars forget, it seems to me, that our enjoyment of the great works of literature depends more upon the depth of our sympathy than upon our understanding. The trouble is that very few of their laborious explanations stick in the memory. The mind drops them as a branch drops its overripe fruit. It is possible to know a flower, root and stem and all, and all the processes of growth, and yet to have no appreciation of the flower freshly by bathed in heaven's dew. Again and again I ask impatiently, "Why concern myself with these explanations and hypotheses?" They fly hither and thither in my thought like blind birds beating the air with ineffectual wings. I do not mean to object to a thorough knowledge of the famous works we read. I object only to the interminable comments and bewildering criticisms that teach but one thing: there are as many opinions as there are men. But when a great scholar like Professor Kittredge interprets what the master said, it is "as if new sight were given to the blind." He brings back Shakespeare, the poet.

There are, however, times when I long to sweep away half the things I am expected to learn; for the overtaxed mind cannot enjoy the treasure it has secured at the greatest cost. It is impossible, I think, to read in one day four or five different books in different languages and consisting of widely different subjects, and not lose sight of the very ends for which one reads.

There are, however, times when I long to sweep away half the things I am expected to learn; for the overtaxed mind cannot enjoy the treasure it has secured at the greatest cost. It is impossible, I think, to read in one day four or five different books in different languages and consisting of widely different subjects, and not lose sight of the very ends for which one reads. When one reads hurriedly and nervously, having in mind written tests and examinations, one's brain becomes encumbered with a lot of choice bric-a-brac for which there seems to be little use. At the present time my mind is so full of heterogeneous matter that I almost despair of ever being able to put it in order. Whenever I enter the region that was the kingdom of my mind, I feel like the proverbial bull in the china shop. A thousand odds and ends of knowledge come crashing about my head like hailstones, and when I try to escape them, theme-goblins and college nixies of all sorts pursue me, until I wish—oh, may I be forgiven the wicked wish that I might smash the idols I came to worship.

But the examinations are the chief bugbears of my college life. Although I have faced them many times and cast them down and made them bite the dust, yet they rise again and menace me with pale looks, until like Bob Acres I feel my courage oozing out of my finger ends. The days before these ordeals take place are spent in cramming your mind with mystic formula and indigestible dates—unpalatable diets, until you wish that those books and science and you were buried in the depths of the sea.

But the examinations are the chief bugbears of my college life. Although I have faced them many times and cast them down and made them bite the dust, yet they rise again and menace me with pale looks, until like Bob Acres I feel my courage oozing out of my finger ends.

At last the dreaded hour arrives, and you are a favoured being indeed if you feel prepared, and are able at the right time to call to your standard thoughts that will aid you in that supreme effort. It happens too often that your trumpet call is unheeded. It is most perplexing and exasperating that just at the moment when you need your memory and a nice sense of discrimination, these faculties take to themselves wings and fly away. The facts you have garnered with such infinite trouble invariably fail you at a pinch.

"Give a brief account of Huss and his work." Huss? Who was he and what did he do? The name looks strangely familiar. You ransack your budget of historic facts much as you would hunt for a bit of silk in a ragbag. You are sure it is somewhere in your mind near the top—you saw it there the other day when you were looking up the beginnings of the Reformation. But where is it now? You fish out all manner of odds and ends of knowledge—revolutions, schisms, massacres, systems of government; but Huss—where is he? You are amazed at all the things you know which are not on the examination paper. In desperation you seize the budget and dump everything out, and there in a corner is your man, serenely brooding on his own private thought, unconscious of the catastrophe which he has brought upon you.

"Give a brief account of Huss and his work." Huss? Who was he and what did he do? The name looks strangely familiar. You ransack your budget of historic facts much as you would hunt for a bit of silk in a ragbag. You are sure it is somewhere in your mind near the top—you saw it there the other day when you were looking up the beginnings of the Reformation.

Just then the proctor informs you that the time is up.

With a feeling of intense disgust you kick the mass of rubbish into a corner and go home, your head full of revolutionary schemes to abolish the divine right of professors to ask questions without the consent of the questioned.

It comes over me that in the last two or three pages of this chapter I have used figures which will turn the laugh against me. Ah, here they are—the mixed metaphors mocking and strutting about before me, pointing to the bull in the china shop assailed by hailstones and the bugbears with pale looks, an unanalysed species! Let them mock on. The words describe so exactly the atmosphere of jostling, tumbling ideas I live in that I will wink at them for once, and put on a deliberate air to say that my ideas of college have changed.

While my days at Radcliffe were still in the future, they were encircled with a halo of romance, which they have lost; but in the transition from romantic to actual I have learnt many things I should never have known had I not tried the experiment.

While my days at Radcliffe were still in the future, they were encircled with a halo of romance, which they have lost; but in the transition from romantic to actual I have learnt many things I should never have known had I not tried the experiment. One of them is the precious science of patience, which teaches us that we should take our education as we would take a walk in the country, at a leisurely pace; our minds hospitably open to impressions of every sort. Such knowledge floods the soul unseen with a soundless tidal wave of deepening thought. "Knowledge is power." Rather, knowledge is happiness, because to have knowledge—broad, deep knowledge—is to know true ends from false, and lofty things from low. To know the thoughts and deeds that have marked man's progress is to feel the great heartthrobs of humanity through the centuries; and if one does not feel in these pulsations a heavenward striving, one must indeed be deaf to the harmonies of life.

□

21

I have thus far sketched the events of my life, but I have not shown how much I have depended on books not only for pleasure and for the wisdom they bring to all who read, but also for that knowledge which comes to others through their eyes and their ears. Indeed, books have meant so much more in my education than in that of others that I shall go back to the time when I began to read.

I read my first connected story in May, 1887, when I was seven years old, and from that day to this I have devoured everything in the shape of a printed page that has come within the reach of my hungry finger tips. As I have said, I did not study regularly during the early years of my education; nor did I read according to rules.

At first I had only a few books in raised print—"readers" for beginners, a collection of stories for children, and a book about the earth called "Our World." I think that was all; but I read them over and over, until the words were so worn and pressed I could scarcely make them out. Sometimes Miss Sullivan read to me, spelling into my hand little stories and poems that she knew I would understand; but I preferred reading myself to being read to, because I liked to read again and again the things that pleased me.

It was during my first visit to Boston that I really began to read in good earnest. I was permitted to spend a part of each day in the Institution library, and to wander from bookcase to bookcase, and take down whatever book my fingers lighted upon. And read I did, whether I understood one word in ten or two words on a page. The words themselves fascinated me; but I took no conscious account of what I read. My mind must, however, have been very impressionable at that period, for it retained many words and whole sentences, about the meaning of which I had not the faintest clue; and afterwards, when I began to talk and write, these words and sentences would flash out quite naturally, so that my friends wondered at the richness of my vocabulary. I must have read parts of many books (in those early days I think I never read any one book through) and a great deal of poetry in this uncomprehending way, until I discovered "Little Lord Fauntleroy," which was the first book of any consequence I read understandingly.

One day my teacher found me in a corner of the library poring over the pages of "The Scarlet Letter." I was then about eight years old. I remember she asked me if I liked little Pearl, and explained some of the words that had puzzled me. Then she told me that she had a beautiful story about a little boy which she was sure I should like better than "The Scarlet Letter." The name of the story was "Little Lord Fauntleroy," and she promised to read it to me the following summer. But we did not begin the story

One day my teacher found me in a corner of the library poring over the pages of "The Scarlet Letter." I was then about eight years old. I remember she asked me if I liked little Pearl, and explained some of the words that had puzzled me. Then she told me that she had a beautiful story about a little boy which she was sure I should like better than "The Scarlet Letter."

until August; the first few weeks of my stay at the seashore were so full of discoveries and excitement that I forgot the very existence of books. Then my teacher went to visit some friends in Boston, leaving me for a short time.

When she returned almost the first thing we did was to begin the story of "Little Lord Fauntleroy." I recall distinctly the time and place when we read the first chapters of the fascinating child's story. It was a warm afternoon in August. We were sitting together in a hammock which swung from two solemn pines at a short distance from the house. We had hurried through the dish-washing after luncheon, in order that we might have as long an afternoon as possible for the story. As we hastened through the long grass towards the hammock, the grasshoppers swarmed about us and fastened themselves onto our clothes, and I remember that my teacher insisted upon picking them all off before we sat down, which seemed to me an unnecessary waste of time. The hammock was covered with pine needles, for it had not been used while my teacher was away. The warm sun shone on the pine trees and drew out all their fragrance. The air was balmy, with a tang of the sea in it. Before we began the story Miss Sullivan explained to me the things that she knew I would not understand, and as we read on she explained the

When she returned almost the first thing we did was to begin the story of "Little Lord Fauntleroy." I recall distinctly the time and place when we read the first chapters of the fascinating child's story. It was a warm afternoon in August. We were sitting together in a hammock which swung from two solemn pines at a short distance from the house.

unfamiliar words. At first there were many words I did not know, and the reading was constantly interrupted; but as soon as I thoroughly comprehended the situation, I became too eagerly absorbed in the story to notice mere words, and I am afraid I listened impatiently to the explanations that Miss Sullivan felt to be necessary. When her fingers were too tired to spell another word, I had for the first time a keen sense of my deprivations. I took the book in my hands and tried to feel the letters with an intensity of longing that I can never forget.

Afterwards, at my eager request, Mr. Anagnos had this story embossed, and I read it again and again, until I almost knew it by heart; and all through my childhood "Little Lord Fauntleroy" was my sweet and gentle companion. I have given these details at the risk of being tedious, because they are in such vivid contrast with my vague, mutable and confused memories of earlier reading.

Afterwards, at my eager request, Mr. Anagnos had this story embossed, and I read it again and again, until I almost knew it by heart; and all through my childhood "Little Lord Fauntleroy" was my sweet and gentle companion. I have given these details at the risk of being tedious, because they are in such vivid contrast with my vague, mutable and confused memories of earlier reading.

From "Little Lord Fauntleroy" I date the beginning of my true interest in books. During the next two years I read many books at my home and on my visits to Boston. I cannot remember what they all were, or in what order I read them; but I know that among them were "Greek Heroes,"

La Fontaine's "Fables," Hawthorne's "Wonder Book," "Bible Stories," Lamb's "Tales from Shakespeare," "A Child's History of England" by Dickens, "The Arabian Nights," "The Swiss Family Robinson," "The Pilgrim's Progress," "Robinson Crusoe," "Little Women," and "Heidi," a beautiful little story which I afterwards read in German. I read them in the intervals between study and play with an ever-deepening sense of pleasure. I did not study nor analyse them—I did not know whether they were well written or not; I never thought about style or authorship. They laid their treasures at my feet, and I accepted them as we accept the sunshine and the love of our friends. I loved "Little Women" because it gave me a sense of kinship with girls and boys who could see and hear. Circumscribed as my life was in so many ways, I had to look between the covers of books for news of the world that lay outside my own.

I did not care especially for "The Pilgrim's Progress," which I think I did not finish, or for the "Fables." I read La Fontaine's "Fables" first in an English translation, and enjoyed them only in a half-hearted fashion. Later I read the book again in French, and I found that in spite of the vivid word-pictures and the wonderful mastery of language, I liked it no better.

I did not care especially for "The Pilgrim's Progress," which I think I did not finish, or for the "Fables." I read La Fontaine's "Fables" first in an English translation, and enjoyed them only in a half-hearted fashion. Later I read the book again in French, and I found that in spite of the vivid word-pictures and the wonderful mastery of language, I liked it no better. I do not know why it is, but stories in which animals are made to talk and act like human beings have never appealed to me very strongly. The ludicrous caricatures of the animals occupy my mind to the exclusion of the moral.

Then, again, La Fontaine seldom, if ever, appeals to our highest moral sense. The highest chords he strikes are those of reason and self-love. Through all the fables runs the thought that man's morality springs wholly from self-love, and that if that self-love is directed and restrained by reason, happiness must follow. Now, so far as I can judge, self-love is the root of all evil; but, of course, I may be wrong, for La Fontaine had greater opportunities of observing men than I am ever likely to have. I do not object so much to the cynical and satirical fables as to those in which momentous truths are taught by monkeys and foxes.

But I love "The Jungle Book" and "Wild Animals I Have Known." I feel a genuine interest in the animals themselves, because they are real animals and not caricatures of men. One sympathises with their loves and hatreds, laughs over their comedies, and weeps over their tragedies. And if they point a moral, it is so subtle that we are not conscious of it.

But I love "The Jungle Book" and "Wild Animals I Have Known." I feel a genuine interest in the animals themselves, because they are real animals and not caricatures of men. One sympathises with their loves and hatreds, laughs over their comedies, and weeps over their tragedies. And if they point a moral, it is so subtle that we are not conscious of it.

My mind opened naturally and joyously to a conception of antiquity. Greece, particularly the ancient Greece, exercised a mysterious fascination over me. In my fancy the pagan gods and goddesses still walked on earth and talked face to face with men, and in my heart I secretly built shrines to those I loved best. I knew and loved the whole tribe of nymphs and heroes and demigods—no, not quite all, for the cruelty and greed of Medea and Jason were too monstrous to be forgiven, and I used to wonder why the gods permitted them to do wrong and then punished them for their wickedness. The mystery is still unsolved. I often wonder how:

> God can dumbness keep
> While Sin creeps grinning through His house of Time.

It was the "Iliad" that made Greece my paradise. I was familiar with the story of Troy before I read it in the original, and consequently had little difficulty in making the Greek words surrender their treasures after I had passed the borderland of grammar. Great poetry, whether written in Greek or in English, needs no other interpreter than a responsive heart. Would that the host of those who make the great works of the poets odious by their analysis, impositions and laborious comments might learn this simple truth! It is not necessary that one should be able to define every word and give it its principal parts and its grammatical position in the sentence in order to understand and appreciate a fine

It was the "Iliad" that made Greece my paradise. I was familiar with the story of Troy before I read it in the original, and consequently had little difficulty in making the Greek words surrender their treasures after I had passed the borderland of grammar. Great poetry, whether written in Greek or in English, needs no other interpreter than a responsive heart.

poem. I know my learned professors have found greater riches in the "Iliad" than I shall ever find; but I am not avaricious. I am content that others should be wiser than I. But with all their wide and comprehensive knowledge, they cannot measure their enjoyment of that splendid epic, nor can I. When I read the finest passages of the "Iliad", I am conscious of a soul-sense that lifts me above the narrow, cramping circumstances of my life. My physical limitations are forgotten—my world lies upwards, the length and the breadth and the sweep of the heavens are mine!

The word-painting of Virgil is wonderful sometimes; but his gods and men move through the scenes of passion and strife and pity and love like the graceful figures in an Elizabethan mask, whereas in the "Iliad" they give three leaps and go on singing.

My admiration for the "Aeneid" is not so great, but it is none the less real. I read it as much as possible without the help of notes or dictionary, and I always like to translate the episodes that please me especially. The word-painting of Virgil is wonderful sometimes; but his gods and men move through the scenes of passion and strife and pity and love like the graceful figures in an Elizabethan mask, whereas in the "Iliad" they give three leaps and go on singing. Virgil is serene and lovely like a marble Apollo in the moonlight. Homer is a beautiful, animated youth in the full sunlight with the wind in his hair.

How easy it is to fly on paper wings! From "Greek Heroes" to the "Iliad" was not one day's journey, nor was it altogether pleasant. One could have travlled round the world many times while I trudged my weary way through the labyrinthine mazes of grammars and dictionaries, or fell into those dreadful pitfalls called examinations, set by schools and colleges for the confusion of those who seek knowledge. I suppose this sort of Pilgrim's Progress was justified by the end; but it seemed interminable to me, in spite of the pleasant surprises that met me now and then at a turn in the road.

I began to read the Bible long before I could understand it. Now it seems strange to me that there should have been a time when my spirit was deaf to its wondrous harmonies; but I remember well a rainy Sunday morning when, having nothing else to do, I begged my cousin to read me a story out of the Bible. Although she did not think I should understand, she began to spell into my hand the story of Joseph and his brothers. Somehow it failed to interest me. The unusual language and repetition made the story seem unreal and far away in the land of Canaan, and I fell asleep and wandered off to the land of Nod, before the brothers came with the coat of many colours unto the tent of Jacob and told their wicked lie! I cannot understand why the stories of the Greeks should have been so full of charm for me, and those of the Bible so devoid of interest, unless it was that I had made the acquaintance of several Greeks in Boston and been inspired by their enthusiasm for the stories of their country; whereas I had not met a single Hebrew or Egyptian, and therefore

I began to read the Bible long before I could understand it. Now it seems strange to me that there should have been a time when my spirit was deaf to its wondrous harmonies; but I remember well a rainy Sunday morning when, having nothing else to do, I begged my cousin to read me a story out of the Bible.

concluded that they were nothing more than barbarians, and the stories about them were probably all made up, which hypothesis explained the repetitions and the queer names. Curiously enough, it never occurred to me to call Greek patronymics "queer."

But how shall I speak of the glories I have since discovered in the Bible? For years I have read it with an ever-broadening sense of joy and inspiration; and I love it as I love no other book. Still there is much in the Bible against which every instinct of my being rebels, so much that I regret the necessity which has compelled me to read it through from beginning to end. I do not think that the knowledge which I have gained of its history and sources compensates for the unpleasant details it has forced upon my attention. For my part, I wish, with Mr. Howells, that the literature of the past might be purged of all that is ugly and barbarous in it, although I should object as much as anyone to having these great works weakened or falsified.

But how shall I speak of the glories I have since discovered in the Bible? For years I have read it with an ever-broadening sense of joy and inspiration; and I love it as I love no other book. Still there is much in the Bible against which every instinct of my being rebels, so much that I regret the necessity which has compelled me to read it through from beginning to end.

There is something impressive and awful in the simplicity and terrible directness of the book of Esther. Could there be anything more dramatic than the scene in which Esther stands before her wicked lord? She knows her life is in his hands; there is no one to protect her from his wrath. Yet, conquering her woman's fear, she approaches him, animated by the noblest patriotism, having but one thought: "If I perish, I perish; but if I live, my people shall live."

The story of Ruth, too—how Oriental it is! Yet how different is the life of these simple country folks from that of the Persian capital! Ruth is so loyal and gentle-hearted; we cannot help loving her, as she stands with the reapers amid the waving corn. Her beautiful, unselfish spirit shines out like a bright star in the night of a dark and cruel age. Love like Ruth's, love which can rise above conflicting creeds and deep-seated racial prejudices, is hard to find in the world.

The story of Ruth, too—how Oriental it is! Yet how different is the life of these simple country folks from that of the Persian capital! Ruth is so loyal and gentle-hearted; we cannot help loving her, as she stands with the reapers amid the waving corn. Her beautiful, unselfish spirit shines out like a bright star in the night of a dark and cruel age.

The Bible gives me a deep, comforting sense that "things seen are temporal, and things unseen are eternal."

I do not remember a time since I have been capable of loving books that I have not loved Shakespeare. I cannot tell exactly when I began Lamb's "Tales from Shakespeare"; but I know that I read them at first with a child's understanding and a child's wonder. "Macbeth" seems to have impressed me most. One reading was sufficient to stamp every detail of the story upon my memory forever. For a long time the ghosts and witches pursued me even into Dreamland. I could see, absolutely see, the dagger and Lady Macbeth's little white hand—the dreadful stain was as real to me as to the grief-stricken queen.

I read "King Lear" soon after "Macbeth," and I shall never forget the feeling of horror when I came to the scene in which Gloster's eyes are put out. Anger seized me, my fingers refused to move, I sat rigid for one long moment, the blood throbbing in my temples, and all the hatred that a child can feel concentrated in my heart.

I must have made the acquaintance of Shylock and Satan about the same time, for the two characters were long associated in my mind. I remember that I was sorry for them. I felt vaguely that they could not be good even if they wished to, because no one seemed willing to help them or to give them a fair chance. Even now I cannot find it in my heart to condemn them utterly. There are moments when I feel that the Shylocks, the Judases, and even the Devil, are broken spokes of the great wheel of good which shall in due time be made whole.

I read "King Lear" soon after "Macbeth," and I shall never forget the feeling of horror when I came to the scene in which Gloster's eyes are put out. Anger seized me, my fingers refused to move, I sat rigid for one long moment, the blood throbbing in my temples, and all the hatred that a child can feel concentrated in my heart.

It seems strange that my first reading of Shakespeare should have left me so many unpleasant memories. The bright, gentle, fanciful plays—the ones I like best now—appear not to have impressed me at first, perhaps because they reflected the habitual sunshine and gaiety of a child's life. But "there is nothing more capricious than the memory of a child: what it will hold, and what it will lose."

I have since read Shakespeare's plays many times and

know parts of them by heart, but I cannot tell which of them I like best. My delight in them is as varied as my moods. The little songs and the sonnets have a meaning for me as fresh and wonderful as the dramas. But, with all my love for Shakespeare, it is often weary work to read all the meanings into his lines which critics and commentators have given them. I used to try to remember their interpretations, but they discouraged and vexed me; so I made a secret pact with myself not to try any more. This pact I have only just broken in my study of Shakespeare under Professor Kittredge. I know there are many things in Shakespeare, and in the world, that I do not understand; and I am glad to see veil after veil lift gradually, revealing new realms of thought and beauty.

Next to poetry I love history. I have read every historical work that I have been able to lay my hands on, from a catalogue of dry facts and dryer dates to Green's impartial, picturesque "History of the English People"; from Freeman's "History of Europe" to Emerton's "Middle Ages." The first book that gave me any real sense of the value of history was Swinton's "World History," which I received on my thirteenth birthday. Though I believe it is no longer considered valid, yet I have kept it ever since as one of my treasures. From it I learnt how the races of men spread from land to land and built great cities, how a few great rulers, earthly Titans, put everything under their feet,

Next to poetry I love history. I have read every historical work that I have been able to lay my hands on, from a catalogue of dry facts and dryer dates to Green's impartial, picturesque "History of the English People"; from Freeman's "History of Europe" to Emerton's "Middle Ages."

and with a decisive word opened the gates of happiness for millions and closed them upon millions more: how different nations pioneered in art and knowledge and broke ground for the mightier growths of coming ages; how civilisation underwent as it were, the holocaust of a degenerated age, and rose again, like the Phoenix, among the nobler sons of the North; and how by liberty, tolerance and education the great and the wise have opened the way for the salvation of the whole world.

In my college reading I have become somewhat familiar with French and German literature. The German puts strength before beauty, and truth before convention, both in life and in literature. There is a vehement, sledge-hammer vigour about everything that he does. When he speaks, it is not to impress others, but because his heart would burst if he did not find an outlet for the thoughts that burn in his soul.

In my college reading I have become somewhat familiar with French and German literature. The German puts strength before beauty, and truth before convention, both in life and in literature. There is a vehement, sledge-hammer vigour about everything that he does. When he speaks, it is not to impress others, but because his heart would burst if he did not find an outlet for the thoughts that burn in his soul.

Then, too, there is a fine reserve in German literature which I like; but its chief glory is the recognition I find in it of the redeeming potency of woman's self-sacrificing love. This thought pervades all German literature and is mystically expressed in Goethe's "Faust":

All things transitory
But as symbols are sent.
Earth's insufficiency
Here grows to event.
The indescribable
Here it is done.
The Woman Soul leads us upward and on!

Of all the French writers that I have read, I like Moliere and Racine the best. There are fine things in Balzac and passages in Merimee which strike one like a keen blast of sea air. Alfred de Musset is impossible! I admire Victor Hugo—I appreciate his genius, his brilliancy, his romanticism; though he is not one of my literary passions. But Hugo and Goethe and Schiller and all great poets of all great nations are interpreters of eternal things, and my spirit reverently follows them into the regions where Beauty and Truth and Goodness are one.

I am afraid I have written too much about my book-friends, and yet I have mentioned only the authors I love most; and from this fact one might easily suppose that my circle of friends was very limited and undemocratic, which would be a very wrong impression.

I am afraid I have written too much about my book-friends, and yet I have mentioned only the authors I love most; and from this fact one might easily suppose that my circle of friends was very limited and undemocratic, which would be a very wrong impression. I like many writers for many reasons—Carlyle for his ruggedness and scorn of shams; Wordsworth, who teaches the oneness of man and Nature; I find an exquisite pleasure in the oddities and surprises of Hood, in Herrick's quaintness and the palpable scent of lily and rose in his verses. I like Whittier for his enthusiasms and moral rectitude. I knew him personally and the gentle remembrance of our friendship doubles the pleasure I have in reading his poems. I love Mark Twain—who does not? The gods, too, loved him and put into his heart all manner of wisdom; then, fearing lest he should become a pessimist, they spanned his mind with a rainbow of love and faith. I like Scott for his freshness, dash and large honesty. I love all writers whose minds, like Lowell's, bubble up in the sunshine of optimism—fountains of joy and good will, with occasionally a splash of anger, and here and there a healing spray of sympathy and pity.

In a word, literature is my Utopia. Here I am not disfranchised. No barrier of the senses shuts me out from the sweet, gracious discourse of my book-friends. They talk to me without embarrassment or awkwardness. The things I have learnt and the things I have been taught seem of ridiculously little importance compared with their "large loves and heavenly charities."

□

22

I trust that my readers have not concluded from the preceding chapter on books that reading is my only pleasure; my pleasures and amusements are many and varied.

More than once in the course of my story I have referred to my love of the country and out-of-door sports. When I was quite a little girl, I learned to row and swim, and during the summer when I am at Wrentham, Massachusetts, I almost live in my boat. Nothing gives me greater pleasure than to take my friends out rowing when they visit me. Of course, I cannot guide the boat very well. Someone usually sits in the stern and manages the rudder while I row. Sometimes, however, I go rowing without the rudder. It is fun to try to steer by the scent of water grasses and lilies, and of bushes that grow on the shore. I use oars with leather bands, which keep them in position in the oarlocks, and I know by the resistance of the water when the oars are evenly poised. In the same manner I can also tell when I am pulling against the current. I like to contend with winds and waves. What can be more exhilarating than to make your staunch little boat, obedient to your will and muscle, go skimming lightly over glistening, tilting waves, and to feel the steady, imperious surge of the water!

I also enjoy canoeing, and I suppose you will smile when I say that I especially like it on moonlight nights. I cannot, it is true, see the moon climb up the sky behind the pines and steal softly across the heavens, making a shining path for us to follow; but I know she is there, and as I lie back among the pillows and put my hand in the water, I fancy that I feel the shimmer of her garments as she passes. Sometimes a daring little fish slips between my fingers, and often a pond-lily presses shyly against my hand. Frequently, as we emerge from the shelter of a cove or inlet, I am suddenly conscious of the spaciousness of the air about me. Luminous warmth seems to enfold me. Whether it comes from the trees which have been heated by the sun, or from the water, I can never discover. I have had the same strange sensation even in the heart of the city. I have felt it on cold, stormy days and at night. It is like the kiss of warm lips on my face.

My favourite amusement is sailing. In the summer of 1901 I visited Nova Scotia, and had opportunities such as I had not enjoyed before of making the acquaintance of the ocean. After spending a few days in Evangeline's country, about which Longfellow's beautiful poem has woven a spell of enchantment, Miss Sullivan and I went to Halifax, where we remained for the

My favourite amusement is sailing. In the summer of 1901 I visited Nova Scotia, and had opportunities such as I had not enjoyed before of making the acquaintance of the ocean. After spending a few days in Evangeline's country, about which Longfellow's beautiful poem has woven a spell of enchantment, Miss Sullivan and I went to Halifax, where we remained for the greater part of the summer.

greater part of the summer. The harbour was our joy, our paradise. What glorious sails we had to Bedford Basin, to McNabb's Island, to York Redoubt, and to the Northwest Arm! And at night what soothing, wondrous hours we spent in the shadow of the great, silent men-of-war. Oh, it was all so interesting, so beautifull The memory of it is a joy forever.

One day we had a thrilling experience. There was a regatta in the Northwest Arm, in which the boats from the different warships were engaged. We went in a sail-boat along with many others to watch the races. Hundreds of little sail-boats swung to and fro close by, and thc sca was calm. When the races were over, and we turned our faces homewards, one of the parties noticed a black cloud drifting in from the sea, which grew and spread and thickened until it covered the whole sky. The wind rose and the waves chopped angrily at unseen barriers. Our little boat confronted the gale fearlessly; with sails spread and ropes taut, she seemed to sit upon the wind. One moment she swirled in the billows and in the next she sprung upwards on a gigantic wave, only to be driven down with angry howl and hiss. Down came the mainsail. Tacking and jibbing, we wrestled with opposing winds that drove us from side to side with impetuous fury. Our hearts beat fast, and our hands trembled with excitement, not

One day we had a thrilling experience. There was a regatta in the Northwest Arm, in which the boats from the different warships were engaged. We went in a sail-boat along with many others to watch the races. Hundreds of little sail-boats swung to and fro close by, and the sea was calm.

fear, for we had the hearts of Vikings and we knew that our skipper was master of the situation. He had steered through many a storm with firm hand and sea-wise eye. As they passed us, the large craft and the gunboats in the harbour saluted and the seamen shouted applause for the master of the only little sail-boat that ventured out into the storm. At last, cold, hungry and weary, we reached our pier.

I spent the last summer in one of the loveliest nooks of one of the most charming villages in New England. Wrentham, Massachusetts, is associated with nearly all of my joys and sorrows. For many years Red Farm, by King Philip's Pond, the home of Mr. J. E. Chamberlin and his family, was my home. I remember with deepest gratitude the kindness of these dear friends and the happy days I spent with them. The sweet companionship of their children meant much to me. I joined in all their sports and rambles through the woods and frolics in the water. The prattle of the little ones and their pleasure in the stories I told them of elf and gnome, of hero and wily bear are pleasant things to remember. Mr. Chamberlin initiated me into the mysteries of tree and wild-flower, until with the little ear of love I heard the flow of sap in the oak, and saw the sun glint from leaf to leaf. Thus it is that:

I spent the last summer in one of the loveliest nooks of one of the most charming villages in New England. Wrentham, Massachusetts, is associated with nearly all of my joys and sorrows. For many years Red Farm, by King Philip's Pond, the home of Mr. J. E. Chamberlin and his family, was my home.

Even as the roots shut in the darksome earth,
Share in the tree-top's joyance, and conceive
Of sunshine and wide air and winged things,
By sympathy of Nature, so did I
Give evidence of things unseen.

It seems to me that there is in each of us a capacity to comprehend the impressions and emotions which have been experienced by mankind from the beginning. Each individual has a subconscious memory of the green earth and murmuring waters, and blindness and deafness cannot rob him of this gift from past generations. This inherited capacity is a sort of sixth sense—a soul-sense which sees, hears, feels, all in one.

I have many tree friends in Wrentham. One of them, a splendid oak, is the special pride of my heart. I take all my other friends to see this king-tree. It stands on a bluff overlooking King Philip's Pond, and those who are wise in tree lore say it must have stood there eight hundred or a thousand years. There is a tradition that under this tree King Philip, the heroic Indian chief, gazed his last on earth and sky.

I have many tree friends in Wrentham. One of them, a splendid oak, is the special pride of my heart. I take all my other friends to see this king-tree. It stands on a bluff overlooking King Philip's Pond, and those who are wise in tree lore say it must have stood there eight hundred or a thousand years.

I had another tree friend, gentle and more approachable than the great oak—a linden that grew in the dooryard at Red Farm. One afternoon, during a terrible thunderstorm, I felt a tremendous crash against the side of the house and knew, even before they told me, that the linden had fallen.

We went out to see the hero that had withstood so many tempests, and it wrung my heart to see him prostrate who had mightily striven and was now mightily fallen.

But I must not forget that I was going to write about last summer in particular. As soon as my examinations were over, Miss Sullivan and I hastened to this green nook, where we have a little cottage on one of the three lakes for which Wrentham is famous. Here the long, sunny days were mine, and all thoughts of work and college and the noisy city were thrust into the background. In Wrentham we caught echoes of what was happening in the world—war, alliance, social conflict. We heard of the cruel, unnecessary fighting in the far-away Pacific, and learnt of the struggles going on between capital and labour. We knew that beyond the border of our Eden men were making history by the sweat of their brows when they might better make a holiday. But we little heeded these things. These things would pass away; here were lakes and woods and broad daisy-starred fields and sweet-breathed meadows, and they shall endure forever.

But I must not forget that I was going to write about last summer in particular. As soon as my examinations were over, Miss Sullivan and I hastened to this green nook, where we have a little cottage on one of the three lakes for which Wrentham is famous. Here the long, sunny days were mine, and all thoughts of work and college and the noisy city were thrust into the background.

People who think that all sensations reach us through the eye and the ear have expressed surprise that I should notice any difference, except possibly the absence of pavements, between walking in city streets and in country roads. They forget that my whole body is alive to the conditions about me. The rumble and roar of the city smite the nerves of my face, and I feel the ceaseless tramp of an unseen multitude, and the dissonant tumult frets my spirit. The grinding of heavy wagons on hard pavements and the monotonous clangour of machinery are all the more torturing to the nerves if one's attention is not diverted by the panorama that is always present in the noisy streets to people who can see.

In the country one sees only Nature's fair works, and one's soul is not saddened by the cruel struggle for mere existence that goes on in the crowded city. Several times I have visited the narrow, dirty streets where the poor live, and I grow hot and indignant to think that good people should be content to live in fine houses and become strong and beautiful, while others are condemned to live in hideous, sunless tenements and grow ugly, withered and cringing.

In the country one sees only Nature's fair works, and one's soul is not saddened by the cruel struggle for mere existence that goes on in the crowded city. Several times I have visited the narrow, dirty streets where the poor live, and I grow hot and indignant to think that good people should be content to live in fine houses and become strong and beautiful, while others are condemned to live in hideous, sunless tenements and grow ugly, withered and cringing. The children who crowd these grimy alleys, half-clad and underfed, shrink away from your outstretched hand as if from a blow. Dear little creatures, they crouch in my heart and haunt me with a constant sense of pain. There are men and women, too, all gnarled and bent out of shape. I have felt their hard, rough hands and realised what an endless struggle their existence must be—no more than a series of scrimmages, thwarted attempts to do something. Their life seems an immense disparity between effort and opportunity. The sun and the air are God's free gifts to all we say, but are they so? In yonder city's dingy alleys the sun shines not, and the air is foul. Oh, man, how dost thou forget and obstruct thy brother man, and say, "Give us this day our daily bread," when he has none? Oh, would that men would leave the city, its splendour and its tumult and its gold, and return to wood and field and simple, honest living! Then would their children grow stately as noble trees and their thoughts sweet and pure as wayside flowers. It is impossible not to think of all this when I return to the country after a year of work in town.

What a joy it is to feel the soft, springy earth under my feet once more, to follow grassy roads that lead to ferny brooks where I can bathe my fingers in a cataract of rippling notes, or to clamber over a stone wall into green fields that tumble and roll and climb in riotous gladness!

What a joy it is to feel the soft, springy earth under my feet once more, to follow grassy roads that lead to ferny brooks where I can bathe my fingers in a cataract of rippling notes, or to clamber over a stone wall into green fields that tumble and roll and climb in riotous gladness!

Next to a leisurely walk I enjoy a "spin" on my tandem bicycle. It is splendid to feel the wind blowing in my face and the springy motion of my iron steed. The rapid rush through the air gives me a delicious sense of strength and buoyancy, and the exercise makes my pulses dance and my heart sing.

Whenever it is possible, my dog accompanies me on a walk or ride or sail. I have had many dog friends—huge mastiffs, soft-eyed spaniels, wood-wise setters and honest, homely bull terriers. At present the lord of my affections is one of these bull terriers. He has a long pedigree, a crooked tail and the drollest "phiz" in the entire dogdom. My dog friends seem to understand my limitations, and always keep close beside me when I am alone. I love their affectionate ways and the eloquent wag of their tails.

Whenever it is possible, my dog accompanies me on a walk or ride or sail. I have had many dog friends—huge mastiffs, soft-eyed spaniels, wood-wise setters and honest, homely bull terriers. At present the lord of my affections is one of these bull terriers. He has a long pedigree, a crooked tail and the drollest "phiz" in the entire dogdom.

When a rainy day keeps me indoors, I amuse myself after the manner of other girls. I like to knit and crochet; I read in the happy-go-lucky way I love, here and there a line; or perhaps I play a game or two of checkers or chess with a friend. I have a special board on which I play these games. The squares are cut out, so that the men stand in them firmly. The black checkers are flat and the white ones curved on top. Each checker has a hole in the middle in which a brass knob can be placed to distinguish the king from the commons. The chessmen are of two sizes, the white larger than the black, so that I have no trouble in following my opponent's manoeuvres by moving my hands lightly over the board after a play. The jar made by shifting the men from one hole to another tells me when it is my turn.

If I happen to be all alone and in an idle mood, I play a game of solitaire, of which I am very fond. I use playing cards marked in the upper right-hand corner with Braille symbols which indicate the value of the card.

If there are children around, nothing pleases me so much as to frolic with them. I find even the smallest child excellent company, and I am glad to say that children usually like me. They lead me about and show me the things they are interested in. Of course the little ones cannot spell on their fingers; but I manage to read their lips. If I do not succeed they resort to dumb charades. Sometimes I make a mistake and do the wrong thing. A burst of childish laughter greets my blunder, and the pantomime begins all over again. I often tell them stories or teach them a game, and the winged hours depart and leave us good and happy.

If there are children around, nothing pleases me so much as to frolic with them. I find even the smallest child excellent company, and I am glad to say that children usually like me. They lead me about and show me the things they are interested in. Of course the little ones cannot spell on their fingers; but I manage to read their lips.

Museums and art stores are also sources of pleasure and inspiration. Doubtless it will seem strange to many that the hand unaided by sight can feel action, sentiment, beauty in the cold marble; and yet it is true that I derive genuine pleasure from touching great works of art. As my finger tips trace the lines and curves, they discover the thought and emotion which the artist has portrayed. I can feel in the faces of gods and heroes hate, courage and love, just as I can detect them in living faces I am permitted to touch. I feel in Diana's posture the grace and freedom of the forest and the spirit that tames the mountain lion and subdues the fiercest passions. My soul delights in the repose and gracious curves of the Venus; and in Barr's bronzes the secrets of the jungle are revealed to me.

A medallion of Homer hangs on the wall of my study, conveniently low, so that I can easily reach it and touch the beautiful, sad face with loving reverence. How well I know each line in that majestic brow tracks of life and bitter evidences of struggle and sorrow; those sightless eyes seeking, even in the cold plaster, for the light and the blue skies of his beloved Hellas, but seeking in vain; that beautiful mouth, firm and true and tender. It is the face of a poet, and of a man acquainted with sorrow. Ah, how well I understand his deprivation—the perpetual night in which he dwelt:

A medallion of Homer hangs on the wall of my study, conveniently low, so that I can easily reach it and touch the beautiful, sad face with loving reverence. How well I know each line in that majestic brow tracks of life and bitter evidences of struggle and sorrow; those sightless eyes seeking, even in the cold plaster, for the light and the blue skies of his beloved Hellas, but seeking in vain; that beautiful mouth, firm and true and tender.

O dark, dark, amid the blaze of noon,
Irrecoverably dark, total eclipse
Without all hope of day!

In imagination I can hear Homer singing, as he gropes

his way from camp to camp with unsteady, hesitating steps —singing of life, of love, of war, of the splendid achievements of a noble race. It was a wonderful, glorious song, and it won the blind poet an immortal crown, the admiration of all ages.

I sometimes wonder if the hand is not more sensitive to the beauties of sculpture than the eye. I should think the wonderful rhythmical flow of lines and curves could be more subtly felt than seen. Be this as it may, I know that I can feel the heart-throbs of the ancient Greeks in their marble gods and goddesses.

I sometimes wonder if the hand is not more sensitive to the beauties of sculpture than the eye. I should think the wonderful rhythmical flow of lines and curves could be more subtly felt than seen. Be this as it may, I know that I can feel the heart-throbs of the ancient Greeks in their marble gods and goddesses.

Another pleasure, which comes more rarely than the others, is going to the theatre. I enjoy having a play described to me while it is being acted on the stage far more than reading it, because then it seems as if I were living in the midst of stirring events. It has been my privilege to meet a few great actors and actresses who have the power of witching you so much that you forget time and place and live again in the romantic past. I have been permitted to touch the face and costume of Miss Ellen Terry as she impersonated our ideal of a queen; and there was about her that divinity that hedges the most sublime woe. Beside her stood Sir Henry Irving, wearing the symbols of kingship; and there was majesty of intellect in his every gesture and attitude and the royalty that subdues and overcomes in every line of his sensitive face. In the king's face, which he wore as a mask, there was a remoteness and inaccessibility of grief which I shall never forget.

I also know Mr. Jefferson. I am proud to count him among my friends. I go to see him whenever I happen to be where he is acting. The first time I saw him act was while at school in New York. He played "Rip Van Winkle." I had often read the story, but I had never felt the charm of Rip's slow, quaint, kind ways as I did in the play. Mr. Jefferson's, beautiful, pathetic representation quite carried me away with delight. I have a picture of old Rip in my fingers which they will never lose. After the play Miss Sullivan took me to see him behind the scenes, and I felt his curious garb and his flowing hair and beard. Mr. Jefferson let me touch his face so that I could imagine how he looked on waking from that strange sleep of twenty years, and he showed me how poor old Rip staggered to his feet.

I also know Mr. Jefferson. I am proud to count him among my friends. I go to see him whenever I happen to be where he is acting. The first time I saw him act was while at school in New York. He played "Rip Van Winkle." I had often read the story, but I had never felt the charm of Rip's slow, quaint, kind ways as I did in the play. Mr. Jefferson's, beautiful, pathetic representation quite carried me away with delight.

I have also seen him in "The Rivals." Once while I was calling on him in Boston he acted out the most striking parts of "The Rivals" for me. The reception-room where we sat served as a stage. He and his son seated themselves at the big table, and Bob Acres wrote his challenge. I followed all his movements with my hands, and caught the drollery of his blunders and gestures in a way that would have been impossible had it all been spelled to me. Then they rose to fight the duel, and I followed the swift thrusts and parries of the swords and the wavering of poor Bob as his courage oozed out at his finger ends. Then the great actor gave his coat a hitch and his mouth a twitch, and in an instant I was in the village of Falling Water and felt Schneider's shaggy head against my knee. Mr. Jefferson recited the best dialogues of "Rip Van Winkle," in which the tear came close upon the smile. He asked me to indicate as far as I could the gestures and action that should go with the lines. Of course, I have no sense whatever of dramatic action, and could make only random guesses; but with masterful art he suited the action to the word. The sigh of Rip as he murmurs, "Is a man so soon forgotten when he is gone?", the dismay with which he searches for dog and gun after his long sleep, and his comical irresolution over signing the contract with Derrick—all these seem to be right out of life itself; that is, the ideal life, where things happen as we think they should.

I remember well the first time I went to the theatre. It was twelve years ago. Elsie Leslie, the little actress, was in Boston, and Miss Sullivan took me to see her in "The Prince and the Pauper." I shall never forget the ripple of alternating joy and woe that ran through that beautiful little play, or the wonderful child who acted it.

I remember well the first time I went to the theatre. It was twelve years ago. Elsie Leslie, the little actress, was in Boston, and Miss Sullivan took me to see her in "The Prince and the Pauper." I shall never forget the ripple of alternating joy and woe that ran through that beautiful little play, or the wonderful child who acted it. After the play I was permitted to go behind the scenes and meet her in her royal costume. It would have been hard to find a lovelier or more lovable child than Elsie, as she stood with a cloud of golden hair floating over her shoulders, smiling brightly, showing no signs of shyness or fatigue, though she had been playing to an immense audience. I was only just learning to speak, and had previously repeated her name until I could say it perfectly. Imagine my delight when she understood the few words I spoke to her and without hesitation stretched her hand to greet me.

Is it not true, then, that my life with all its limitations touches at many points the life of the World Beautiful? Everything has its wonders, even darkness and silence, and I learn that whatever state I may be in, therein to be content.

Sometimes, it is true, a sense of isolation enfolds me like a cold mist as I sit alone and wait at life's shut gate. Beyond it there is light, and music, and sweet companionship; but I may not enter. Silent, pitiless Fate bars the way. Fain would I question his imperious decree, for my heart is still undisciplined and passionate; but my tongue will not utter the bitter, futile words that rise to my lips, and they fall back into my heart like unshed tears. Silence sits immense upon my soul. Then comes hope with a smile and whispers, "There is joy in self-forgetfulness." So I try to make the light in others' eyes my sun, the music in others' ears my symphony, the smile on others' lips my happiness.

□

23

Would that I could enrich this sketch with the names of all those who have ministered to my happiness! Some of them would be found written in our literature and dear to the hearts of many, while others would be wholly unknown to most of my readers. But their influence, though it escapes fame, shall live immortal in the lives that have been sweetened and ennobled by it. Those are red-letter days in our lives when we meet people who thrill us like a fine poem, people whose handshake is brimful of unspoken sympathy, and whose sweet, rich natures impart to our eager, impatient spirits a wonderful restfulness which, in its essence, is divine. The perplexities, irritations and worries that have absorbed us pass like unpleasant dreams, and we wake up to see with new eyes and hear with new ears the beauty and harmony of God's real world. The solemn nothings that fill our everyday life blossom suddenly into bright possibilities. In a word, while such friends are near us we feel that all is well. Perhaps we never saw them before, and they may never cross our life's path again; but the influence of their calm, mellow natures is a libation poured upon our discontent, and we feel its healing touch, as the ocean feels the mountain stream and freshens up its brine.

I have often been asked, "Do not people bore you?" I do not quite understand what that means. I suppose the calls of the stupid and curious, especially of newspaper reporters, are always inopportune. I also dislike people who try to talk down to my understanding. They are like people who when walking with you try to shorten their steps to suit yours; the hypocrisy in both cases is equally exasperating.

The hands of those I meet are dumbly eloquent to me. The touch of some hands is impertinent. I have met people so empty of joy, that when I clasped their frosty finger tips, it seemed as if I were shaking hands with a northeast storm. Again, there are those whose hands have sunbeams in them, so that their grasp warms my heart. It may be only the clinging touch of a child's hand; but there is as much potential sunshine in it for me as there is in a loving glance for others. A hearty handshake or a friendly letter gives me genuine pleasure.

The hands of those I meet are dumbly eloquent to me. The touch of some hands is impertinent. I have met people so empty of joy, that when I clasped their frosty finger tips, it seemed as if I were shaking hands with a northeast storm.

I have many far-off friends whom I have never seen. Indeed they are so many that I have often been unable to reply to their letters; but I wish to say here that I am always grateful for their kind words, however insufficiently I acknowledge them.

I count it as one of the sweetest privileges of my life to have known and conversed with many men of genius. Only those who knew Bishop Brooks can appreciate the joy that his friendship was to those who possessed it. As a child I loved to sit on his knee and clasp his great hand with one of mine, while Miss Sullivan spelled into the other his beautiful words about God and the spiritual world. I heard him with a child's wonder and delight. My spirit could not reach up to his, but he gave me a real sense of joy in life, and I never left him without carrying away a fine thought that grew in beauty and depth of meaning as I grew. Once, when I was puzzled about why there were so many religions, he said: "There is one universal religion, Helen—the religion of love. Love your Heavenly Father with your whole heart and soul, love every child of God as much as ever you can, and remember that the possibilities of good are greater than the possibilities of evil; and you have the key to Heaven." And his life was a happy illustration of this great truth. In his noble soul love and widest knowledge were blended with faith that had become insight. He saw

God in all that liberates and lifts,
In all that humbles, sweetens and consoles.

Bishop Brooks taught me no special creed or dogma; but he impressed upon my mind two great ideas—the fatherhood of God and the brotherhood of man, and made me feel that these truths underlie all creeds and forms of worship. God is love, God is our Father, we are His children; therefore the darkest clouds will break and though right be worsted, wrong shall not triumph.

Bishop Brooks taught me no special creed or dogma; but he impressed upon my mind two great ideas—the fatherhood of God and the brotherhood of man, and made me feel that these truths underlie all creeds and forms of worship.

I am too happy in this world to think much about the future, except to remember that I have cherished friends awaiting me there in God's beautiful kingdom. In spite of the lapse of years, they seem so close to me that I should not think it strange if at any moment they should clasp my hand and speak words of endearment as they used to before they went away.

Since Bishop Brooks died I have read the Bible through as also some philosophical works on religion, among them Swedenborg's "Heaven and Hell" and Drummond's "Ascent of Man," and I have found no creed or system more soul-satisfying than Bishop Brooks creed of love. I knew Mr. Henry Drummond, and the memory of his strong, warm hand-clasp is like a benediction. He was the most sympathetic of companions. He knew so much and was so genial that it was impossible to feel dull in his presence.

I remember well the first time I saw Dr. Oliver Wendell Holmes. He had invited Miss Sullivan and me to call on him one Sunday afternoon. It was early in the spring, just after I had learned to speak. We were shown at once to his library where we found him seated in a big armchair by an open fire which glowed and crackled on the hearth, thinking, he said, of other days.

I remember well the first time I saw Dr. Oliver Wendell Holmes. He had invited Miss Sullivan and me to call on him one Sunday afternoon. It was early in the spring, just after I had learned to speak. We were shown at once to his library where we found him seated in a big armchair by an open fire which glowed and crackled on the hearth, thinking, he said, of other days.

"And listening to the murmur of the River Charles," I suggested.

"Yes," he replied, "the Charles has many dear associations for me." There was an odour of print and leather in the room which told me that it was full of books, and I stretched out my hand instinctively to find them. My fingers lighted upon a beautiful volume of Tennyson's poems, and when Miss Sullivan told me what it was I began to recite:

Break, break, break
On thy cold grey stones, O sea!

But I stopped suddenly. I felt tears on my hand. I had made my beloved poet weep, and I was greatly distressed. He made me sit in his armchair, while he brought different interesting things for me to examine, and at his request I recited "The Chambered Nautilus," which was then my favourite poem. After that I saw Dr. Holmes many times and learnt to love the man as well as the poet.

But I stopped suddenly. I felt tears on my hand. I had made my beloved poet weep, and I was greatly distressed. He made me sit in his armchair, while he brought different interesting things for me to examine, and at his request I recited "The Chambered Nautilus," which was then my favourite poem. After that I saw Dr. Holmes many times and learnt to love the man as well as the poet.

One beautiful summer day, not long after my meeting with Dr. Holmes, Miss Sullivan and I visited Whittier in his quiet home on the Merrimac. His gentle courtesy and quaint speech won my heart. He had a book of his poems in raised print from which I read "In School Days." He was delighted that I could pronounce the words so well, and said that he had no difficulty in understanding me. Then I asked many questions about the poem, and read his answers by placing my fingers on his lips. He said he was the little boy in the poem, and that the girl's name was Sally, and more which

I have forgotten. I also recited "Laus Deo," and as I spoke the concluding verses, he placed in my hands a statue of a slave from whose crouching figure the fetters were falling, even as they fell from Peter's limbs when the angel led him forth out of prison. Afterwards we went into his study, and he wrote his autograph for my teacher ["With great admiration of thy noble work in releasing from bondage the mind of thy dear pupil, I am truly thy friend. John J. Whittier"] and expressed his admiration of her work, saying to me, "She is thy spiritual liberator." Then he led me to the gate and kissed me tenderly on my forehead. I promised to visit him again the following summer, but he died before the promise was fulfilled.

Dr. Edward Everett Hale is one of my very oldest friends. I have known him since I was eight, and my love for him has increased with my years. His wise, tender sympathy has been the source of support of Miss Sullivan and me in times of trial and sorrow, and his strong hand has helped us over many rough places; and what he has done for us he has done for thousands of those who have difficult tasks to accomplish. He has filled the old skins of dogma with the new wine of love, and shown men what it is to believe, live and be free. We have seen his teachings beautifully expressed in his own

I have known him since I was eight, and my love for him has increased with my years. His wise, tender sympathy has been the source of support of Miss Sullivan and me in times of trial and sorrow, and his strong hand has helped us over many rough places; and what he has done for us he has done for thousands of those who have difficult tasks to accomplish.

life—love of country, kindness to the least of his brethren, and a sincere desire to live upward and onward. He has been a prophet and an inspirer of men and a mighty doer of the Word, the friend of his entire race—God bless him!

I have already written of my first meeting with Dr. Alexander Graham Bell. Since then I have spent many happy days with him at Washington and at his beautiful home in the heart of Cape Breton Island, near Baddeck, the village made famous by Charles Dudley Warner's book. Here in Dr. Bell's laboratory, or in the fields on the shore of the great Bras d'Or, I have spent many delightful hours listening to what he had to tell me about his experiments, and helping him fly kites by means of which he expects to discover the laws that shall govern the future air-ship. Dr. Bell is proficient in many fields of science, and has the art of making every subject he touches interesting including even the most abstruse theories. He makes you feel that if you only had a little more time, you, too, might be an inventor. He has a humorous and poetic side, too. His dominating passion is his love for children. He is never quite as happy as when he has a little deaf child in his arms. His labour on behalf of the deaf will live on and bless generations of children yet to come; and we love him alike for what he himself has achieved and for what he has evoked in others.

I have already written of my first meeting with Dr. Alexander Graham Bell. Since then I have spent many happy days with him at Washington and at his beautiful home in the heart of Cape Breton Island, near Baddeck, the village made famous by Charles Dudley Warner's book.

During the two years I spent in New York I had many

opportunities of talking with distinguished people whose names I had often heard, but whom I had never expected to meet. I met most of them for the first time in the house of my good friend, Mr. Laurence Hutton. It was a great privilege to visit him and dear Mrs. Hutton in their lovely home, and see their library and read the beautiful sentiments and bright thoughts that their gifted friends had written for them. It has been truly said that Mr. Hutton has the faculty of bringing out in everyone the best thoughts and kindest sentiments. One does not need to read "A Boy I Knew" to understand him—the most generous, sweet-natured boy I ever knew, a good friend in all sorts of weather, who traces the footprints of love in the life of dogs as well as in that of his fellowmen.

During the two years I spent in New York I had many opportunities of talking with distinguished people whose names I had often heard, but whom I had never expected to meet. I met most of them for the first time in the house of my good friend, Mr. Laurence Hutton.

Mrs. Hutton is a true and tried friend. I owe to her much of all that I hold sweetest and much of all that I hold most precious. She has often advised and helped me in my progress through college. When I find my work particularly difficult and discouraging, she writes me letters that make me feel glad and brave; for she is one of those from whom we learn that one painful duty fulfilled makes the next plainer and easier.

Mr. Hutton introduced me to many of his literary friends, the greatest of whom are Mr. William Dean Howells and Mark Twain. I also met Mr. Richard Watson Gilder and Mr. Edmund Clarence Stedman. I also knew Mr. Charles

Dudley Warner, the most delightful of story-tellers and the most beloved friend, whose sympathy was so broad that it may be truly said of him, that he loved all living things and his neighbour as himself. Once Mr. Warner brought to see me the dear poet of the woodlands—Mr. John Burroughs. They were all gentle and sympathetic and I felt the charm of their manner as much as I had felt the brilliance of their essays and poems. I could not keep pace with all these literary folk as they glanced from subject to subject and entered into deep dispute, or made conversation sparkle with epigrams and happy witticisms. I was like little Ascanius, who followed with unequal steps the heroic strides of Aeneas on his march towards mighty destinies. But they spoke many gracious words to me. Mr. Gilder told me about his moonlight journeys across the vast desert to the Pyramids, and in a letter he wrote me he made his mark under his signature deep in the paper so that I could feel it. This reminds me that Dr. Hale used to give a personal touch to his letters to me by pricking his signature in Braille. I read from Mark Twain's lips one or two of his good stories. He has his own way of thinking, saying and doing everything. I can feel the twinkle of his eye in his handshake. Even while he utters his cynical wisdom in an indescribably droll voice,

I was like little Ascanius, who followed with unequal steps the heroic strides of Aeneas on his march towards mighty destinies. But they spoke many gracious words to me. Mr. Gilder told me about his moonlight journeys across the vast desert to the Pyramids, and in a letter he wrote me he made his mark under his signature deep in the paper so that I could feel it.

he makes you feel that his heart is a tender Iliad of human sympathy.

There are a host of other interesting people I met in New York: Mrs. Mary Mapes Dodge, the beloved editor of St. Nicholas, and Mrs. Riggs (Kate Douglas Wiggin), the sweet author of "Patsy." I received from them gifts that have the gentle concurrence of the heart, books containing their own thoughts, soul-illumined letters, and photographs that I love to have described again and again. But there is not enough space to mention all my friends, and indeed there are things about them hidden behind the wings of cherubim, things too sacred to set forth in cold print. It is with hesitancy that I have spoken even of Mrs. Laurence Hutton.

There are a host of other interesting people I met in New York: Mrs. Mary Mapes Dodge, the beloved editor of St. Nicholas, and Mrs. Riggs (Kate Douglas Wiggin), the sweet author of "Patsy." I received from them gifts that have the gentle concurrence of the heart, books containing their own thoughts, soul-illumined letters, and photographs that I love to have described again and again.

I shall mention only two other friends. One is Mrs. William Thaw, of Pittsburgh, whom I have often visited in her home, Lyndhurst. She is always doing something to make someone happy, and her generosity and wise counsel have never failed my teacher and me in all the years we have known her.

To the other friend I am also deeply indebted. He is well known for the powerful hand with which he guides vast enterprises, and his wonderful abilities have gained for him the respect of all. Kind to everyone, he goes about doing good, silent and unseen. Again I touch upon the circle of honoured names I must not mention; but I would fain acknowledge his generosity and affectionate interest which make it possible for me to go to college.

Thus it is that my friends have made the story of my life. In a thousand ways they have turned my limitations into beautiful privileges, and enabled me to walk serene, content and happy in the shadow cast by my deprivation.

□□□